RANDOM HOUSE
SNOW DAY
CROSSWORDS

edited by
STANLEY
NEWMAN

**Random House
Puzzles & Games**

SPECIAL SALES

Random House Puzzles & Games books are available at special discounts
for bulk purchases for sales promotions or premiums. Special editions,
including personalized covers, excerpts of existing books, and corporate
imprints, can be created in large quantities for special needs.
For more information, contact Random House Special Markets at 800-800-3246.

---

1 POSTSCRIPTS

by Randolph Ross

ACROSS

1 Brit's raincoat
4 Complain
8 Nicolas of *Moonstruck*
12 Verdi opera
13 Mild cigar
15 Quite excited
16 Early Beatles song
18 Math. course
19 "__ you so"
20 Boards Amtrak
22 "Sausage" anagram
25 Hard work
26 Biblical song
31 Bottle tops
34 Dessert wedge
35 __ Gay
36 Have a bug
37 You may mind them
40 Come out first
41 First-quality
43 College in NYC
44 On the briny
45 Artful liar
49 Casino implement
50 WWII camps
54 In the cellar
58 Bowling-alley button
59 Auto rod
60 Freud's line
63 *Let's Make a Deal* choice
64 Ancient Aegean region
65 In a snit
66 Wallet fillers

67 Beatty and Buntline
68 Hear a case

DOWN

1 Spritzes
2 Bolivian bye-bye
3 Draft orders
4 20% of MXXV
5 Draft order
6 Mirthful Martha
7 Immediately if not sooner
8 Majorcan language
9 Culture commencer
10 Enter
11 Meringue ingredients
12 Samoan capital
14 __ sorts (peevish)
17 Harem quarters
21 Six Flags attractions
23 Open spaces
24 Director Kazan
27 __ Park, NJ
28 They may be exchanged
29 Nastase of tennis
30 Carvey or Delany
31 Yokum's creator
32 Snobs' put-on
33 Ballet move
37 Step on it
38 Archaeological expeditions
39 Bow out
42 Columbo's cases
44 Minimally
46 Giraffe's cousin
47 Tutoring session
48 Asian apparel
51 Early American tycoon
52 Madison VP
53 Eye problem
54 Pedestal part
55 Former Nebraska senator
56 Spiny houseplant
57 Actress Daly
61 El __ (Spanish hero)
62 Gives birth to

OPINION OPINION

by Eric Albert

ACROSS

1 Get the hang of
7 Like some victories
15 C to C, e.g.
16 Defeat
17 START OF A QUIP
19 Wield an axe
20 No longer new
21 Hoop star Thurmond
22 Razor's asset
24 Addams uncle
26 PART 2 OF QUIP
31 Slalom curve
32 Thwart a thrust
33 Pours down
35 Day-care denizen
36 Bird call
38 '60s hairstyle
42 Western resort
44 League rule
45 Crowded, initially
48 PART 3 OF QUIP
51 Orion's trade
53 Ex-Yugoslav leader
54 Wine region
55 Fly rapidly
57 "__ the ramparts . . ."
60 END OF QUIP
65 Honored one
66 Turns of phrase
67 New one in town
68 Astaire/ Rogers classic

DOWN

1 Sweater muncher
2 Sign of strain
3 Worried state
4 Little bit
5 Night before
6 Safe place
7 Unpartnered
8 Roman poet
9 Gerbil, maybe
10 __ Lanka
11 Holy symbols
12 Chip in
13 Feigns feelings
14 Puts off
18 "Aha!"
22 Swamp dweller
23 Finish with the dishes
24 Wacky Wilson
25 Poet's nighttime
26 Inclined (to)
27 One opposed
28 Biblical boat
29 Sky sign
30 Watering hole
34 Authority
36 *Mermaids* star
37 Opp. of vert.
39 Follies name
40 Controlled
41 Be in the red
43 Friend of Tarzan
44 Drill insert
45 Shoulder garments
46 Head headlong for
47 In a road show
49 Big name in elevators
50 Silly-willy
52 Jeweled headdress
55 Fancy party
56 Lustful look
57 "Oops!"
58 Madame Bovary
59 Take five
61 Col. superior
62 Joplin opus
63 Altar vow
64 Tout's offering

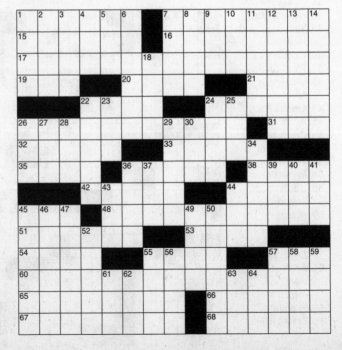

3 ROCK CONCERT

by Bob Lubbers

ACROSS

1 Western actor Jack
5 Makeshift store
10 Straw vote
14 Name for a poodle
15 Japanese-American
16 Part of B&O
17 How geologists take things?
19 Tach readings
20 Noisy napper
21 Park art
23 Ignore the script
26 GI entree
27 Highway hangings
30 John __ Passos
32 Upper crust
35 Refuses to
36 Genderless
38 Mannerless man
39 Vane dir.
40 Protective coats
41 __ out a living
42 Half of CIV
43 Pencil's place
44 Govt. agents
45 Sci-fi weapon
47 Choose: Abbr.
48 Civil-rights leader Medgar
49 Fumble one's speech
51 Lively dances
53 Wealthy woman
56 Don't act up
60 "Nova" anagram
61 Geologist's assay gear?
64 Frying medium
65 What you see
66 Twist out of shape
67 Some brothers
68 Wyoming range
69 Collar insert

DOWN

1 Gees' preceders
2 Elsa's dad
3 Continental prefix
4 Itinerant worker
5 Traffic tie-up
6 Foil material
7 "__ live and breathe!"
8 NBA team
9 Eating plans
10 Mine entrance
11 Geologist's favorite song?
12 Pie ingredient
13 Investor's bane
18 Bright shades
22 Sound-alikes of a sort
24 High standards
25 More daring, like a geologist?
27 "Peachy keen!"
28 Old Aegean region
29 Geologist's encouraging words?
31 Brosnan role
33 Bet acceptor
34 Perfect places
36 Classical prefix
37 Make a mistake
40 Shoulder movement
44 *Maude* and *Rhoda*
46 Four-legged Kenyans
48 TVA power
50 Send simoleons
52 *The Beverly Hillbillies* star
53 Broad valley
54 Roundish shape
55 Frost
57 Get __ on the back
58 Ms. Miles
59 Catch sight of
62 *The __ in the Hat*
63 In olden days

by S.N.

ACROSS

1 Oil initials
5 __ Hari
9 Drink deeply
14 Canadian prov.
15 *Jeopardy!* name
16 Excessive
17 Klinger portrayer
18 Undaffy
19 Aircraft walkway
20 Comes home, sort of
22 Scout Carson
23 Wedding-column word
24 "If __ a Hammer"
26 Road "beetles"
29 __ *bene*
31 Absolute ruler
32 Schnozz
33 Pirate Hall-of-Famer
36 1980 Wimbledon winner
37 Midwestern hockey team
38 __ *Wonderful Life*
39 Manor master
40 Troubleless
41 Badminton boundary
42 A little change
43 Graceful tree
44 Shake up
45 Antebellum Confederacy
50 Kiddie-lit elephant
53 Hawaiian holiday spot
54 '60s spy airplane
55 Flabbergast
56 RBI, e.g.
57 Charlotte et al.
58 Posh
59 Slangy turndown
60 "__ a Lady" (Jones tune)

DOWN

1 Clumsy folk
2 Urban map
3 Raison d'__
4 CBer's need
5 En __ (as a group)
6 Jai __
7 French Revolution event
8 Tree cutter
9 Dennis of *Innerspace*
10 Single thing
11 Paid notices
12 Spoon or joy ending
13 Professional payment
21 Absorbed, as a school subject
22 Writer Capek and director Reisz
25 Saltlike
26 Not arterial
27 British alemaker
28 Keel-rudderpost connectors
29 Replace an old obligation
30 Orchestral member
31 Have nothing __ (get stuck, detective-wise)
32 Makes alluring
33 Varnish ingredient
34 Penn's partner
35 Mercer and Normand
42 Singer Mariah
43 Mrs. Bunker
44 Dizzy's genre
46 Waikiki feast
47 Western state
48 Bird call
49 Cartwright boy
50 Ingot
51 "What a good boy __"
52 Mr. Masterson
53 College at E. Lansing

5 AUTO SUGGESTION

by Donna J. Stone

ACROSS

1 Greek-salad ingredient
5 *Soapdish* star
10 __ of the Roses
14 Court-martial candidate
15 *Unsafe at Any Speed* author
16 Seer's sign
17 Floor model
18 Boston Symphony leader
19 Printing process
20 START OF A QUIP
23 Frome of fiction
25 Morse message
26 Show follower
27 Bud's buddy
28 Sound of shock
32 Old saw
34 Poet's foot
36 "OK with me!"
39 MIDDLE OF QUIP
42 Sea World attraction
43 Spitz sounds
46 Gandhi, e.g.
49 Spirited steed
51 Letters of credit?
52 *Wheel of Fortune* buy
53 Erich __ Stroheim
56 Capp character
58 END OF QUIP
63 Dilatorily
64 Philip Nolan's fate
65 Just around the corner
68 *Dukes of Hazzard* deputy
69 Term-paper need
70 The Fatman's friend
71 Bears' lairs
72 First sign
73 *Kismet* setting

DOWN

1 In thing
2 Flock female
3 Barnum attraction
4 Ho "Hi!"
5 Chest gripper
6 Be idle
7 Lupino and Tarbell
8 Small salamanders
9 Thalia's sister
10 Despicable one
11 It multiplies by dividing
12 Tommy of *Lassie*
13 Cop some Z's
21 MIT grad
22 Hayes or Stern
23 Cotton gin name
24 __ T (perfectly)
29 "I've Got __ in Kalamazoo"
30 Pea product
31 Turkish title
33 Action time
35 Melville character
37 Successor
38 Author Ferber
40 "__ Got a Friend"
41 Slickers and such
44 "The Gold Bug" author
45 Big __, CA
46 Rained hard?
47 Crackers
48 Vegas singer
50 Do away with
54 __ a customer
55 *Six Crises* author
57 Dog star
59 Musical Myra
60 Counterchange
61 Björn opponent
62 Splinter group
66 Alias letters
67 Purchase paperwork: Abbr.

CARRY ALL

by Alex Vaughn

ACROSS

1 Way to address a lady
5 *M*A*S*H* character
10 Exxon's ex-name
14 __ *La Douce*
15 Run off and wed
16 Zhivago's love
17 Mortgage, e.g.
18 Something extra
19 Radiate
20 Joey carrier
23 Bullfight "bravo"
24 Had what __ (measured up)
27 Syrup source
30 Because you were challenged
34 French "one"
35 They kiss
37 Direction, in Durango
38 Neighborhoods
39 Introduction to metrics?
40 Sup at home
41 At __ (wholesale)
42 Visigoths' doing
44 Bard's "before"
45 He really kneads you
46 Actor Beatty
47 *Cheers* star
49 Wine word
51 Matter-of-taste remark
58 Himalayas' home
60 Still in contention
61 Rubik's device
62 Visual signal
63 Sham artist
64 Recline idly
65 Keyed up
66 Makes level
67 Peers at

DOWN

1 Cereal partner
2 Moffo solo
3 Solemn assent
4 Tropical fruit
5 Kind of collision
6 Actor Ray
7 Unprogressive one
8 Each
9 Louvre display
10 Vote in
11 Revered Texan
12 __ Lanka
13 Bran source
21 Spiny houseplants
22 Western Indian
25 Airline-board phrase
26 Wailed
27 Skipped a line
28 __ borealis
29 Ringmaster's word
31 Assumed name
32 They're round and flat
33 Buy a pig in __
36 Rode the bench
37 Lobe's locale
40 Mr. Zimbalist
42 Southwestern capital
43 Dismissals
45 Bird Maoris once hunted
48 Not very secure
50 Repetitive pattern
52 Croat, for one
53 Reebok rival
54 Pizza place?
55 Harbor bobber
56 Well-qualified
57 Solidifies
58 Wide-eyed wonder
59 Imogene's cohort

7 MAP OF THE STARS

by Randolph Ross

ACROSS

1 Former Congressman Aspin
4 __ facto
8 Mr. Waller
12 Clinton's home
14 Touch against
15 *Arsenic and Old Lace* actress
17 "You're __ and don't know it"
18 CIA predecessor
19 *Exodus* hero
21 *Monitor* foe
25 Learner's need
27 Media revenue source
28 Simile center
29 Sushi-bar selections
30 *Cheers* actress
35 *Perry Mason* role
36 *The Big Chill* actress
38 Aid in crime
39 __ for "Apple"
40 Reb inits.
43 All __ (Miller play)
46 Gets rid of
49 Slalom curve
50 Shoe specification
52 Employee's last words
53 Wimbledon winner in '70
58 Golden-__ (senior citizen)
59 Astronomical event
60 One of Jacob's sons
61 Bartlett's abbr.
62 Night spot

DOWN

1 Drank like a cat
2 Scoreboard column
3 Killy, for one
4 Business-letterhead letters
5 Greek letter
6 "My Gal __"
7 Cold capital
8 Like some bottoms
9 Lawyers' org.
10 Sandwich order
11 Germfree
13 Italian wine region
16 Small snake
17 *I __ Fugitive from a Chain Gang*
20 Bitsy preceder
22 Comic actress Gibbs
23 Ore analysis
24 Unwitting dupe
26 Civil War signature
30 __ the city (mayor's bestowal)
31 Sort
32 Let __ (don't touch)
33 Make a clean slate
34 NRC predecessor
35 Equine event
36 Jerry Herman musical
37 Just awful
40 Golf links
41 Was right for
42 Member of 9 Down
44 Silents siren
45 Diver's place
47 "New Look" designer
48 Short news item
51 Author Bombeck
54 Gun the engine
55 Lunch ending
56 As well
57 Where to see Larry King

HEAVEN FOR BID!

by Donna J. Stone

ACROSS

1 Analyzed sentences
7 Clammy
11 Race downhill
14 Pianist de Larrocha
15 Bridge support
16 Groan producer
17 START OF A QUIP
19 Part of SBLI
20 Robert __ Marley
21 Cleanse
23 *Three Men __ Baby*
26 Admitted, with "up"
29 *Scarface* star
30 Last word in fashion
32 Mythical twin
34 Cartoon cat
35 Boss' note
36 MIDDLE OF QUIP
41 Cut out cake
42 Giggle sound
45 Most promptly
49 Tile game
51 Behold, to Brutus
52 Jeweler's measure
54 As a result
55 Mideast nation
57 Tall story?
59 Dos Passos trilogy
60 END OF QUIP
66 Velvet finish
67 Get-up-and-go
68 Crewel tool
69 Drain-cleaner ingredient
70 D'Artagnan prop
71 Whirled

DOWN

1 Pastoral god
2 Inn quaff
3 *6 Rms, __ Vu*
4 Game plan
5 Irish republic
6 Former *Family Feud* host
7 Armless sofa
8 Justice Fortas
9 Framing need
10 Play thing?
11 Inflationary pattern
12 Martial art
13 Atlas features
18 Periodic-table info: Abbr.
22 Montevideo's loc.
23 Campaign name of '36
24 Dundee denial
25 Punctually
27 "... __ saw Elba"
28 St. Paul's feature
31 Ooze
33 March, but not mazurka
35 *The A-Team* star
37 Go for broke
38 Salad cheese
39 Feeling low
40 Restaurateur Toots
43 MIT grad
44 Inflated feeling
45 *Batman Returns*, e.g.
46 *Purple Dust* playwright
47 Gas rating
48 PBS benefactor
49 __ Hari
50 Bring into harmony
53 Alto or bass
56 Tear down
58 Completed the cake
61 Helpful hint
62 *Wheel of Fortune* buy
63 A mean Amin
64 Message to a matador
65 Nancy Drew's boyfriend

9 YES, YES, YES!

by Trip Payne

ACROSS

1 *Casablanca* role
4 Lobster eater's wear
7 Lustrous fabric
13 Pretended to be
16 Geronimo, for one
17 Warn
18 Mine workers
19 Prove false
20 Dry, as wine
22 "This is only __"
23 Haughty one
24 Tissue cell
26 Like some pots
28 Kind of file
32 Hindu chant
35 Males
36 Aware of
37 Does as told
38 Winner's prize
39 Coming next
40 "Whip It" rock group
41 __ and aah
42 __ Creed (religious statement)
43 Rebekah's son
44 Cactus type
46 Not up
48 Mail agcy.
52 Fuel nuggets
55 4/15 org.
56 Floorboard sound
57 Like some inspections
59 Tibetan hideaway
61 Riffled (through)
62 *The Moon and __*
63 Gets narrower
64 Gaming cube
65 Understanding words

DOWN

1 Warms up for a bout
2 Standish stand-in
3 Rumba relative
4 Out of shape
5 Mr. Amin
6 Droopy dog
7 Fish, in a way
8 Bee-related
9 Logically expected event
10 Top level
11 "__ a Lady"
12 Superman's alias
14 Groucho show
15 Ray Charles' commercial backup
21 Social pariah
24 Hunters' org.
25 Offs' opposite
27 __ *gratia artis*
29 Kitty starter
30 British gun
31 Skin feature
32 Manner
33 Burrows and Vigoda
34 St. Petersburg's river
38 Raccoon relative
39 Put on TV
41 CIA forerunner
42 Shrewish type
45 Tacit
47 Nitrate, e.g.
49 "__ evil . . ."
50 Shrivel with heat
51 Some terriers
52 Stable child
53 Draftable person
54 PDQ kin
56 Horn, for one
58 Bradley and McBain
60 1011, to Tacitus

by Mel Rosen

ACROSS

1 __ Romeo
5 Complete victory
10 Not processed
13 Mother of William and Harry
15 Jeweled headpiece
16 Miss. neighbor
17 Newspaper staffer
20 Speedometer's meas.
21 Make (one's way)
22 Knock for a loop
23 "__ Old Cowhand"
25 Tough test
29 Check total
31 Trumpet effect
32 Sixth sense
35 Sperry's partner
36 Changes shades
37 Sault __ Marie, MI
38 Iowan, for one
43 Half and half?
44 Clapton of rock
45 A big jerk
46 Home, in the phone book
47 Chihuahua child
48 Plumed military hats
50 Dry-cleaning worker
52 Lancastrian symbol
53 Inner drive
55 Prefix for focus
57 *Die Fledermaus* subject
60 Carpentry contraption
65 Early gardener
66 Pleasure boat
67 Couldn't stand
68 Round Table address
69 Miller rival
70 Evergreen shrubs

DOWN

1 Hockey star Oates
2 Emulate Daffy
3 Dior, for one
4 *Wheel of Fortune* buy
5 Mr. Musial
6 Department-store staffer
7 Do lunch
8 Poetic preposition
9 Mini-notebook
10 Hiker's risk
11 Manager Felipe
12 Put on notice
14 Dam in Egypt
18 Bivouac quarters
19 "This __ fine how-do-you-do!'"
24 Newsman Roger
26 Beams of light
27 Eat more sensibly
28 Additional
29 Jouster's protection
30 Memorable vessel
33 Office skill, for short
34 Job benefits
39 Carson successor
40 Moran of *Happy Days*
41 Cellar stock
42 Thick-piled rugs
48 Mex. miss
49 Cheap booze
51 Alert color
53 Puts to work
54 Sitarist Shankar
56 Judges of a sort
58 Once more
59 Koppel and Turner
61 Coll. deg.
62 "Xanadu" group
63 Old card game
64 Loft material

11 WATER MUSIC

by Donna J. Stone

ACROSS

1 British buggy
5 Window sticker
10 Bridge charge
14 Old bird
15 Display conspicuously
16 "__ Around" (Beach Boys tune)
17 College courtyard
18 Wagner's father-in-law
19 Loquacious equine
20 Italian water music?
23 Pine product
24 R-V hookup?
25 Texas state tree
28 "So that's your game!"
31 Tire Town, USA
35 Epoch
36 Cantaloupe's cousin
39 Narrow shoe size
40 French water music?
43 Czech river
44 Singer Brewer
45 Sleeve contents?
46 Ball-bearing attractions?
48 Neighbor of Jord.
49 *Gaslight* star
51 Inept sort
53 Wine and dine
54 Chinese water music?
61 Jupiter's alias

62 Michelangelo subject
63 Hardly hyper
65 Sacred cow
66 Cockamamie
67 Raison d'__
68 Scads
69 Vacuum-tube gas
70 Pants part

DOWN

1 Pronto, initially
2 No gentleman
3 *Queen for* __
4 Pavarotti's birthplace
5 Dutch pottery
6 Way out
7 Old Testament kingdom
8 Cooper's tool
9 Baltic natives
10 Faraway place
11 Mythical monster
12 Lascivious look
13 Inc., in Ireland
21 Light weight
22 "Make __ double!"
25 Señorita's shekels
26 Carve a canyon
27 __ cropper (failed)
28 Grate stuff
29 Like Esau
30 Capp character
32 Settle accounts
33 In reserve
34 *Unsafe at Any Speed* author
37 ABA member

38 Horse cousin
41 Bobby Vinton #1 tune
42 Off-limits
47 Lose energy
50 Lots and lots
52 Recruit's NJ home
53 Valhalla VIP
54 Skywalker's teacher
55 Revlon rival
56 Big name in westerns
57 Writer Hunter
58 Producer De Laurentiis
59 Hung up
60 Pound of poetry
61 Dandy's first name?
64 Even so

12 HIGH HOPES

by Shirley Soloway

ACROSS

1 Get away from
7 Colorful shell
14 Footstool
15 New Jersey river
16 Wishful pursuit
18 Gary and Mary
19 *Dallas* matriarch
20 Ottawa's prov.
21 Sword handle
24 Make a choice
28 Clairvoyant ability
30 Slow mover
32 Caviar
33 Bea of vaudeville
35 *One Day at __*
37 Wishful pursuit
41 O'er opposite
42 Expenditure
43 One-third of MCCIII
44 Blossom holder
45 Art, to Antony
48 Mr. Melville
52 Wedding vows
54 Comic Philips
56 "You __ be congratulated!"
58 Mint jelly
60 Wistful pursuit
65 Large wardrobe
66 Is indicative of
67 Hold back
68 Hams it up

DOWN

1 Fuel gas
2 Gets underway
3 The bottom line
4 Pennsylvania sect
5 Hook's nemesis
6 Liberia's lang.
7 Asian inland sea
8 __ out (uses a chute)
9 *L.A. Law* guy
10 Suit grounds
11 Western Indian
12 Slangy refusal
13 Printer's widths
14 Acapulco octet
17 Payback
22 Punching tools
23 Paper sheets
25 Buffalo's lake
26 Robin Cook book
27 Be abundant
29 Evil scheme
31 Turned gooey
34 Self suffix
35 Tooth pros' grp.
36 "__ Little Tenderness"
37 About 2.5 centimeters
38 Old-time Persian
39 Matched set
40 Brat in *Blondie*
46 Fame
47 Strikes down
49 Feudal estate
50 Bandleader Shaw
51 Gets close to
53 Antidrug advice
55 Folk singer Phil
57 Laces up
59 Flue dust
60 A long way off
61 Raw metal
62 Man behind the catcher
63 Commemorative verse
64 Neither masc. nor neut.

13 SO THEY SAY

by Eric Albert

ACROSS

1 Deep black
4 Leading lady Lamarr
8 Borgnine role
14 *Messiah* is one
16 Tooth covering
17 Pedestrian path
18 Unremarkable
19 HOME
21 Fish eggs
22 When Paris sizzles
23 Glimpse
26 Declare openly
28 British baby buggy
32 Farrow of films
33 Scandinavian city
35 *My Favorite Year* star
37 FAMILIARITY
40 Writer Welty
41 Ms. Sommer
42 Unit of energy
43 Checkup
44 Music symbol
46 Lavish attention (on)
47 Ave. crossers
48 Ram's mate
50 MISS
58 Get back
59 One with a marker
60 Chinese philosopher
61 Hungry for company
62 Oscar-winner as Mrs. Kramer
63 Picnic predators
64 Before marriage

DOWN

1 Kid around
2 Pennsylvania port
3 "Voila!"
4 Bookstore section
5 Clean the boards
6 Pickle flavoring
7 __ Ono
8 Cautionary sign
9 100-buck bill
10 Mata __
11 Clips and shells
12 Incline
13 Building extension
15 Towel material
20 Corp. boss
23 Patter provider
24 Crazy Horse, for one
25 Bamboo bruncher
26 Swiss peak
27 Marks a ballot
28 "El Dorado" writer
29 Cowpuncher competition
30 Make aware of
31 Join forces
33 "__ the ramparts..."
34 Get wise
36 Pipe type
38 Piper's son
39 PBJ alternative
45 Leg. title
46 Salami shops
47 Take by force
48 Major happening
49 Walks through water
50 Essential point
51 Composer Stravinsky
52 Recent
53 Pac-10 member
54 Common supplement
55 Kind of collar
56 Dome home zone
57 Kite nemesis
58 *Kidnapped* monogram

14 SECURITY RISK

by Donna J. Stone

ACROSS

1 Dict. abbr.
4 Epsilon follower
8 Coeur d'__, ID
13 Perrins' partner
14 Cheese choice
15 Partonesque
16 START OF A QUIP
19 Calculator ancestor
20 Ale place
21 Sapphire side
22 Make up (for)
24 Citrus cooler
26 Busy as __
27 Napoleon's fate
28 Aftereffect
29 "Cool!" in school
30 Numerical suffix
31 Folklore being
32 MIDDLE OF QUIP
35 Menotti title character
38 Tropical tuber
39 Sine __ non
42 Scads
43 Belgian Congo, today
45 Hair balls?
46 Parker product
47 They may be greased
48 Shearer of *The Red Shoes*
49 '60s dance
51 Short snooze
52 END OF QUIP
55 Take __ at (attempt)
56 Make a buck
57 Vane reading
58 Bedtime reading
59 Eye problem
60 Cherry shade

DOWN

1 Morgiana's master
2 Wrote graffiti
3 Local booster
4 The *Odyssey* character
5 Actor Byrnes
6 Asian philosophy
7 Explosive
8 Superior to
9 Mechanic's job
10 Chef's concentrate
11 Kind of sun
12 Funnyman Philips
17 No longer in style
18 Maureen O'Sullivan role
19 Out of range
22 Skating maneuver
23 Dickens character
25 Go wrong
27 *Sea Hunt* shocker
28 Actor Mineo
30 __ Aviv
31 Exit-ramp word
32 Kid's query
33 Crew-team members
34 Ending for press
35 Audiophile's purchase
36 Cary Grant's '33 co-star
37 Food coloring
39 Malaria medicine
40 Like some movies
41 Urgent letters
43 Ms. Pitts
44 __ *Restaurant*
45 Pain in the neck
47 Reserve
48 Foot wiper
50 Kaiser's counterpart
51 French film
52 Great time, so to speak
53 *Krazy* __
54 Ironic

15 ALPHABETS

by Lois Sidway

ACROSS

1 Way off
4 Orchestral areas
8 Alabama city
13 "Isn't It a __?" ('32 tune)
14 Conversation filler
15 Burger topping
16 Folklore baddie
17 Blind part
18 Shakespearean forest
19 Key letters
22 Actor's quest
23 __ de corps
27 One: Ger.
28 OR personnel
30 Matador's foe
31 Young hog
34 Message from Morris
36 Top bond rating
37 Behave
40 Vane reading
41 A Kentucky Derby prize
42 Postulate
43 "I've Got __ in Kalamazoo"
45 A Bobbsey twin
46 Evildoing
47 Tell
49 Ruse victims
53 Victory sign, to Morse
56 Where you live
59 Matured
60 __ Camera (basis for Cabaret)
61 Western capital
62 Extra

63 Prepare to swallow
64 San Diego baseballer
65 James Bond's alma mater
66 Holyfield stats

DOWN

1 Night's work for Holyfield
2 Awesome hotel lobbies
3 Deli need
4 Car part
5 Eastern religion
6 Thailand export
7 __ precedent
8 Midday TV fare
9 Filled with delight
10 It may be flipped
11 A Stooge
12 Actress Jillian
13 Ice-cream buys
20 Perry White's occupation
21 They'll buy burritos
24 Interstates
25 OPEC delegate
26 Breakfast order
28 Elevated
29 Gets some z's
31 Sloppy brushstroke
32 Be contingent
33 Peyton Place star
34 Western plateau
35 American elk
38 Musical group
39 Like Teflon
44 Painter's need
46 Depress
48 "__ Kangaroo Down, Sport"
49 Word form for "wing"
50 Spud country
51 Furniture designer
52 Henry Higgins' creator
54 British title
55 "__ the sun in the morning . . ."
56 Cleo's cobra
57 Ewe said it
58 Like Mother Hubbard

BODY SOUNDS

by Fred Piscop

ACROSS

1. __ it up (overacts)
5. Wilma's hubby
9. Birch relative
14. Blind as __
15. Like some hair
16. Superman star
17. Ms. Barrett
18. Krugerrand, for one
19. Like some fences
20. TOE
23. Phonograph needles
24. Form of wrestling
25. Gun grp.
28. Ave. crossings
30. Melee starter
33. "Do __ say . . ."
36. Aid partner
39. Pelvic bone
40. EYE
44. Toyota model
45. Fuss
46. Composer Rorem
47. Plain as day
49. Deviate from the course
52. Temp. unit
53. Bridges or Brummell
56. Well-dressed
60. NOSE
64. Barber's offering
66. __ pas (mistake)
67. Hard to believe
68. Navel type
69. Wings: Lat.
70. Thpeak like thith
71. Spiral-shelled creature
72. Legendary apple splitter
73. Greek H's

DOWN

1. Ethereal instruments
2. More or less
3. Macho
4. Stable units
5. Central points
6. Civil disturbances
7. Root or Yale
8. Blew up
9. Jason's craft
10. __ day (2/29)
11. School kid's punishment
12. Cain raiser
13. Richard Skelton
21. Clever chap
22. Author L. __ Hubbard
26. Meet the old grads
27. Gave guns to
29. __ Jose, CA
31. Org. once led by Bush
32. Under the weather
33. Traveled a curved path
34. Italian wine
35. Join the melting pot
37. Milk component
38. Comedian Philips
41. Suffix with drunk or cow
42. Humorist Bill
43. Mr. Rogers
48. Warriors' org.
50. Part of Q&A
51. Turkey-throat feature
54. Allan-__
55. Business as __
57. Genetic feature
58. Oral Roberts U. site
59. Canine's cries
61. Emulating Lucifer
62. Oddball
63. Rink jump
64. Mama pig
65. "What did you say?"

17 NOTTINGHAM REVISITED

by Randolph Ross

ACROSS

1 Skyline sight
6 Some tires
13 __ *Knowledge* ('71 film)
14 Loathed one
16 Nottingham lithographs?
18 Upswing
19 In the matter of
20 Silvery fish
21 Meet with
23 Repressed, with "up"
25 Gin name
26 Nottingham bride?
31 Had a bite
32 Midmonth day
33 Garry and Melba
37 Make a bad pact
39 Hindu heaven
40 Middle of *Macbeth*
41 "__ Be Cruel"
42 Enthusiasm
43 Nottingham gangsters?
46 TV initials
49 Reliever's stat
50 Big __, CA
51 Separates socks
54 Grande and Bravo
56 Mount Snow machine
59 Nottingham merchant?
62 Popular sitcom
63 Palate projections
64 Introvert's trait
65 Like Mr. Universe

DOWN

1 Calcutta clothing
2 Most prim
3 Destitute
4 Hamelin pest
5 Ms. Lanchester
6 Roof holders
7 *Julius Caesar* character
8 Bit of Morse code
9 Like __ (candidly)
10 "Psst!" elative
11 Flood preventative
12 Common sense
13 EMT training
15 Italian wine region

17 Fish hawk
22 Charlie Sheen's brother
24 Comedian's need
26 One of the Bears
27 Suffix for problem
28 Quick-thinking retorts
29 Oliver and Sheree
30 Cuomo's title: Abbr.
34 Auk feature
35 Oklahoma city
36 Undermines
38 Broadcast medium
39 Preceder of "the above"

41 Goes through mitosis
44 Captains of industry
45 Beat on the track
46 V.I. Lenin's land
47 Cheerful sounds
48 Just-picked
52 Deuce beater
53 Exemplar of grace
55 Urban-renewal target
57 Have __ in (influence)
58 Numbered hwy.
60 *A Chorus Line* number
61 Eggs

by S.N.

ACROSS

1 Wants to know
5 Switch positions
9 Purina rival
13 Dalmatian's name
14 Bowling term
15 *Mommie Dearest* name
16 Walk nervously
17 Reddy to sing?
18 Kick in a chip
19 October activity
22 Once around the track
23 Wilm. is there
24 *Wheel of Fortune* purchase
27 Stinky cigar
30 Thrill
35 Entertainer Falana
37 Acapulco gold
38 Made night noises
39 October activity
42 Oblivious to ethics
43 One __ customer
44 Ltr. enclosure
45 Critic, often
46 Divine food
48 Sun. speech
49 __ de cologne
51 Head stroke
53 October activity
61 Notorious Ugandan
62 __ *for the Misbegotten*
63 PDQ, O.R.-style
65 Retail
66 Set-to
67 Ingrain deeply
68 Quite dark
69 Van __, CA
70 Give's partner

DOWN

1 Nile reptile
2 Minor disagreement
3 *Mayor* author
4 Mill output
5 Phone letters
6 It may be free
7 Elm Street name
8 Good judgment
9 Open a crack
10 Actress Anderson
11 Crown of the head
12 Some bills
14 Lathe, e.g.
20 Had been
21 Hurricane of '85
24 Wedding platform
25 __ *Rae*
26 *The Waste Land* poet
28 Hockey Hall-of-Famer
29 "Ya __ have heart . . ."
31 A whole bunch
32 Opera highlights
33 Suffering stress
34 Gardener's device
36 Suburban square?
38 *Colors* star
40 Black or Valentine
41 Director Howard
46 Waikiki wear
47 Travel grp.
50 Larry Storch's *F Troop* role
52 Rec-room piece
53 Sitarist Shankar
54 Prayer ending
55 Eccentricity
56 May event, familiarly
57 Ride for a kid
58 Colleague of Clark and Jimmy
59 Feminine-name ending
60 Pillage
64 "__ end"

by Wayne R. Williams

ACROSS

1 One-time Wimbledon winner
5 Ecology org.
8 Least risky
14 Faster way
16 Said grace
17 Interrupt
18 Stair elements
19 Furry swimmer
20 Most secret
22 Calendar letters
23 Make a choice
25 Australian area
29 Hot tub
30 Turndown vote
31 Jeff Bridges film of '84
32 $2 exacta, e.g.
33 DDE defeated him
34 Life of Riley
35 Gets tiresome
38 Ornery equine
39 Inferno writer
40 Model Macpherson
41 Friday was one
42 __ Ridge, TN
43 Teddy's niece
45 Coral islet
46 Sphere
49 Withdraw
50 Killer whale
51 Act dovish
52 Cattle food
54 Fur tycoon
56 Musical chords
59 Catch up to
61 Tight spot
62 Corporate buyout
63 Overacts
64 Olsen of vaudeville
65 Makes one

DOWN

1 Classy neckwear
2 Pipe down
3 Devon drink
4 Irish Gaelic
5 Author Umberto
6 Virtuousness
7 Env. abbr.
8 Alfalfa form
9 Manilow's record label
10 Basketball maneuver
11 Look over
12 Sun. homily
13 NFL scores
15 Power seats
21 Charlton role
24 Bit of butter
26 To __ (unanimously)
27 The players
28 Leg flexer
32 Morning meal
33 Egyptian cobra
35 Coach Ewbank
36 Ms. Fitzgerald
37 Sir Guinness
38 Major artery
39 Tot service
41 Soup and salad
42 Long paddle
44 Brain, so to speak
45 Contemporary
46 From C to C
47 Flimflammed
48 Drills, e.g.
53 Arrive at
55 Put away
56 Kin of les and der
57 Hit head-on
58 Prefix for metric
60 __ out a living

by Eric Albert

ACROSS

1 Sop ink
5 FDR topic
9 Film sensitivity
14 Tasty tubers
15 __ California
16 Genghis' gang
17 START OF A QUIP
19 Sigourney Weaver film
20 Flagpole topper
21 PART 2 OF QUIP
23 Expects
25 March ender
26 Messy Madison
29 Nasal-sounding
33 Kid around
36 "Oops!"
38 Napoleon, twice
39 Mideast name
40 PART 3 OF QUIP
42 __-de-sac
43 National Zoo attraction
46 Cry like a baby
47 Computer noise
48 Swallow up
50 Peruvian beast
52 Close with force
54 "__, you fool!"
58 PART 4 OF QUIP
63 Price twice
64 Bouquet
65 END OF QUIP
67 Like a lot
68 Immense volume
69 Enthusiastic
70 Some cookies
71 Turn aside
72 All those in favor

DOWN

1 Two, to Revere
2 Legal drama
3 End-all
4 Prufrock's poet
5 Agents' org.
6 Simplicity
7 Trojan War hero
8 House style
9 Invitation to dance
10 Amendment XXIV subject
11 Canal of song
12 Land west of Nod
13 Auto mark
18 Pups and parrots
22 Take a loss in
24 Flat-bottomed boat
27 *Pequod* skipper
28 Fit for a queen
30 Jet-set resort
31 Stick together
32 Short shout
33 Make fun of
34 Zesty spirit
35 Birds do it
37 Allen Ginsberg opus
41 Strong rebuke
44 Tidying tool
45 Eager to hear
47 Pre-overtime amount
49 Low-tech cooler
51 Spanish surrealist
53 Diamond gloves
55 "Wild and crazy" Martin
56 *West Side Story* song
57 "Dear me!"
58 Falls behind
59 Common diet supplement
60 Convertible, maybe
61 Cranny's colleague
62 Jacks, but not Jills
66 Recently arrived

21 FULL OF BEANS

by Eric Albert

ACROSS

1 Mr. Sharif
5 Persian potentate
9 Kind of orange
14 Raging blaze
16 Tony of baseball
17 '70s auto
18 It "keeps on ticking"
19 Tattletales
20 Ewe's partner
21 To some extent
24 Employment aid
28 Baby Snooks portrayer
29 Papergirl's path
31 Mai __ (cocktail)
32 Paper puzzle
33 Circus shooter
34 Likely (to)
35 *On the Town* lyricist
38 Golfer's goal
40 Jacket parts
41 Guns the engine
44 Corn holder
45 "If __ a Rich Man"
46 Bit of salt
47 Unspecified person
49 Exhaust one's creativity
50 Was in front
51 Entity
53 Highly motivated
56 Knee tendon
60 Monk's cloister
61 Avant-garde composer
62 Minnie of Nashville
63 Dampens
64 Bush's alma mater

DOWN

1 Out of synch
2 "O Sole __"
3 Part of ETA
4 Blushing
5 Be frugal
6 Bumper-sticker word
7 Tatum and Carney
8 Med. ins. plan
9 Prose alert
10 Out on __ (vulnerable)
11 Vitality
12 Actress Arden
13 Over easy
15 Church top
20 Brake parts
21 Computer co.
22 New Deal org.
23 Inca conqueror
24 Tarzan's home
25 Concluded
26 Grab forty winks
27 Radio to assemble
29 Ice-T, e.g.
30 __ *Majesty's Secret Service*
33 Like old bathtubs
36 *Thimble Theater* name
37 *Silver Spoons* star
38 *Treasure Island* character
39 Display delight
42 Taper?
43 Avoiding fame
46 Kicks, in a way
48 Berry tree
49 Takes a flier
51 Unornamented
52 Give out
53 Casual topper
54 Justice Fortas
55 Hoop group: Abbr.
56 Take an axe to
57 Call __ day
58 Nada
59 "That's awesome!"

GYM NEIGHBORS

by Wayne R. Williams

ACROSS

1 Puppeteer Lewis
6 Harm, in a way
10 Be up and about
14 More than ready
15 *M*A*S*H* star
16 Painter Joan
17 Sound of a critic?
19 Erelong
20 Sicilian landmark
21 *Superman* villain Luthor
22 Burstyn and Barkin
24 Broker's lots
26 Handle capably
27 Sound of an actor?
30 Be sick
33 Lucy's landlady
36 Entreaties
37 Novelist Levin
38 Heavy sound
39 Toothy displays
40 Map out
41 Make leather
42 Got up
43 Emitted beams
44 Army insect
45 Sound of a ballplayer?
47 Out-and-out
49 Prepare
53 Disarm a bull
55 Squeak curer
57 __ podrida
58 Old lament
59 Sound of an actress?

62 Melancholy
63 Nautical adverb
64 Ike's missus
65 Mineo and Maglie
66 Desires
67 Winter gliders

DOWN

1 Ed Norton's workplace
2 Author Bret
3 Booster rocket
4 Brought back
5 Nettle
6 Stable female
7 *Jeopardy!* name
8 Actress Lupino
9 Portuguese wines
10 T-shirt size
11 Sound of an actress?
12 Tailor's need
13 Howard and Nessen
18 Roy Rogers' real last name
23 Not as many
25 Up to, briefly
26 Hot dog
28 Brouhaha
29 Prime social category
31 "Dies __"
32 Touch down
33 Jazz singer James
34 Comparative word
35 Sound of a Bowery Boy?
39 Smallest city with an NFL team
40 Beethoven's Sixth
42 Mimic
43 Sage of Concord's monogram
46 Eye amorously
48 Fuel-line components
50 *Ghostbusters* goo
51 Spanish hero
52 Walks off with
53 Pats lightly
54 Joyce of *Roc*
55 Author Wister
56 March time
60 Bullring cheer
61 Apt. ad abbr.

ACROSS

1 Act testily
7 Erivan native
15 Bob,
   but not Joe
16 "Misty" start
17 Open an
   envelope
18 Captain
   Stubing's
   command
19 Guys' dates
20 "Our __ your
   gain"
22 Met Life's bus.
23 Computer key
25 Storage unit
26 Yon bloke's
28 In __
   (disheveled)
30 Inn offerings
35 Summer drink
36 Well-executed
37 Just plain
   awful
38 Green-light
   phrase
41 Cookout
   locales
42 Gator's home,
   maybe
43 Free (of)
44 Merlin of TV
45 In unison
46 Sea plea
47 Farrow et al.
48 Know-nothing
   remark
50 Obstinate
   equine
53 Beer holder
55 Vaccine name
58 Perry victory
   site
60 Visigoth
   leader
62 Book's
   edition

63 Saskatchewan's
   capital
64 "Diagnose"
   anagram
65 Donald
   Sutherland's
   kid

DOWN

1 *The Color
   Purple*
   character
2 Barrie barker
3 Theater spots
4 Egg on
5 Oklahoma
   city
6 Ring a bell
7 Green-light
   phrase
8 They're often
   ruled
9 *Z* or *M*

10 Supplements,
   with "out"
11 Catch a crook
12 Even odds
13 __ *for All
   Seasons*
14 Is left with
21 West Indies
   belief
24 Aviator of
   the comics
26 *Duck Soup*
   soloist
27 Optimal
29 Kitten's cries
30 Rose up
31 Buckeyes' sch.
32 Filmdom's
   Zhivago
33 Former
   Governor
   Cuomo
34 Snow gliders

37 Actress
   Cannon
39 Stamping tool
40 Rope feature
45 Musty house's
   need
47 Madame Curie
49 The way
   we word
50 Swiss range
51 Lee of
   cakedom
52 Spud covering
53 "You __ do!"
54 Carefree frolic
56 Reinforce,
   in a way
57 Former
   Chrysler
   category
59 Last part
61 Aiea
   adornment

24 "GEEZ!"

ACROSS

1 Some sandwiches
6 Blue-ribbon event
10 Tijuana cheers
14 __-garde
15 Discourteous
16 Mr. Hackman
17 Rho follower
18 Flash of brilliance
19 Research info
20 Mom's rock-pile admonition?
22 Daredeviltry name
23 Smoke-detector output
24 Mean and nasty
26 Condescended
30 Comb impediment
31 Big apes
32 Application phrase
36 Succotash bean
37 Novelist Rand
38 Sills solo
39 Service holder of a sort
42 *Tobacco Road* family name
44 In this way
45 Simple life
46 It's spotted in the zoo
49 Turin "Ta-ta!"
50 Get an __ effort
51 Antelope city?
57 German capital
58 Forsaken
59 Stan's cohort
60 __-dry (arid)
61 ". . . __ saw Elba"
62 Frosted, in recipes
63 Controversial tree spray
64 "Dagnabbit!"
65 Some votes

DOWN

1 Door fastener
2 Sinful
3 Shankar genre
4 "__ honor, I will do my . . ."
5 Producing plays
6 "__ or foe?"
7 Imported automobiles
8 March 15th, for instance
9 Justifications
10 Angry poet?
11 Go out
12 Go in
13 Mattress name
21 Opposers of 65 Across
25 Beans spiller
26 Knucklehead
27 Buffalo's county
28 __ *Camera* ('55 film)
29 Pesky rebellion leader?
30 __ Clemente, CA
32 Caustic stuff
33 Comic Johnson
34 Appearance
35 Shucker's needs
37 Capp and Capone
40 "*Now* I see!"
41 Stole from
42 Pinocchio, often
43 Save-the-earth science
45 *The __ Winter*
46 __ the Hutt (Lucas character)
47 "__ and his money . . ."
48 "You're __ Hear from Me"
49 Healer
52 Author Ephron
53 *Cosmopolitan* competitor
54 Word of woe
55 Jet-set city
56 Bishops' realms

by Eric Albert

ACROSS

1 Turn away
6 *Pygmalion* playwright
10 Camel feature
14 Resort isle
15 Short note
16 Laos' locale
17 BAR
20 *Joy of Cooking* abbr.
21 Guitar kin, for short
22 Clear a channel
23 Southpaw's sobriquet
26 Joyride
27 Red wood
29 Floor covering
30 Block a broadcast
33 High home
34 Actress Delany
35 Brouhaha
36 BAR
39 Director Kazan
40 Wines and dines
41 *Where's __?* ('70 film)
42 Howard of *Happy Days*
43 Big jerk
44 Dressing table
45 Pretentiously picturesque
46 Puts on the payroll
47 Mr. Kosygin
50 Golfer Woosnam
51 *Murphy Brown* network
54 BAR
58 G&S character
59 Walk out

60 *Lost Horizon* director
61 Pipe part
62 Painter Magritte
63 Makes meals

DOWN

1 Large quantity
2 Love god
3 Prince tune of '84
4 Decline
5 Chou En-__
6 Great __ Mountains National Park
7 "I'm present!"
8 Rock-band gear
9 Punny business
10 Safe place
11 Practiced
12 Flash's foe
13 Top of the head
18 Import tax
19 Border lake
24 *All My Children* character
25 Ad word
26 Hole in your head
27 Silly prank
28 Surprised exclamation
29 Something banned
30 *SNL* alumnus
31 Well-practiced
32 Coral-reef denizen
34 Humdinger
35 Kind of steak
37 Unfaithful one

38 On __ with (equal to)
43 Brought up
44 Trattoria offering
45 Universal truth
46 Rapidity
47 Proposes as a price
48 Spoils of war
49 Sommer of *The Prize*
50 "When the moon __ the seventh house . . ."
52 Tree feature
53 Mineral springs
55 Tin Man's tool
56 Radio regulator: Abbr.
57 __ Paulo

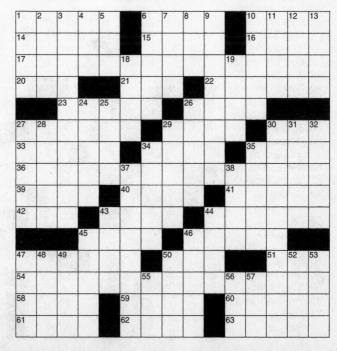

by Trip Payne

ACROSS

1 Syrup source
6 Elbow room
11 Walk like pigeons
14 Vermont town
15 Condor's claw
16 Vane abbr.
17 With 62 Across, a 1991 award winner
19 New-style "Swell!"
20 *Hamlet* phrase
21 *Romeo Must __ Album*
23 British maid
26 Award won by 17 Across
29 Garfield's middle name
31 "For shame!"
32 Bits of butter
33 Hexer's belief
35 React to yeast
38 With 53 Across, 26 Across' awarder
42 Wild guess
43 New Orleans school
46 Woodpile spot
50 Zodiac animal
52 Words of consolation
53 See 38 Across
57 Stash away
58 Mysterious knowledge
59 Poi source
61 Viscount's drink
62 See 17 Across
68 UFO pilots
69 "Oh, hush!"
70 Plumber's prop
71 Anonymous Richard
72 Door joint
73 Barely defeated

DOWN

1 Kittenish sound
2 Gray shade
3 "__ Love You" (Beatles tune)
4 Doyle's inspector
5 Montreal player
6 Mason's assistant
7 Handle roughly
8 *Arabian Nights* name
9 W.'s National Security Advisor, familiarly
10 No __ sight
11 Cannon's name
12 *Cat __ Tin Roof*
13 Sprinkles, in a way
18 Head away
22 Seer's sense
23 Cleveland NBAer
24 Showtime rival
25 "Pretty maids all in __"
27 Of interest to Bartleby
28 Dime-like
30 Rolling stone's lack
34 Mel of baseball
36 Fast flier
37 Needle case
39 Playwright Connelly
40 Norwegian dog
41 Sari wearer
44 Doze (off)
45 Female antelope
46 Hamill or Witt
47 Bit of legalese
48 Box up
49 Genetic letters
51 Change genetically
54 Methuselah's father
55 Hawaiian island
56 Totally outlaw
60 U.S. national flower
63 __ Arbor, MI
64 Smoke, for short
65 Droop down
66 __ out a living
67 Was in first

THREE OF A KIND

ACROSS
1 Slows down
8 Slugger's tool . . .
11 . . . and what it's made of
14 Walter Hickel, for one
15 Cornered
17 Versatile one
19 "Who am __ argue?"
20 HS class
21 Franklin et al.
22 Hunters' wear
25 Grazing land
26 Forearm bones
27 Sounds of relief
29 M. Descartes
31 Word before driver or school
34 Campaign staffer
35 Blazed trails
38 Bogie's Oscar film
41 Fore's opposite
42 Show anger
43 Colorado city
44 *Edward Scissorhands* star
45 Lose rigidity
46 Fast car
49 Circle section
52 Women's mag
56 Jai __
57 Grammy winner Irene
59 Nothing at all
60 Lion
65 Scott hero
66 Like some basements

67 Singer Tillis
68 Stylish, '60s-style
69 Goes over

DOWN
1 Indira's son
2 Fill with delight
3 Baja noshes
4 Pose an issue
5 *King Kong* studio
6 Off one's rocker
7 Traffic tie-up
8 Warsaw Pact member
9 Fitting
10 Punish severely
11 Eve or Elizabeth

12 "You look like you've just __ ghost!"
13 *Steppenwolf* writer
16 Casino furniture
18 Be duplicitous
23 Mock fanfare
24 *Amadeus* playwright
26 Not uniform
28 IHOP freebie
30 Ferber and Best
31 El stop: Abbr.
32 Channels 14 and up
33 After taxes
34 Hole in one
35 Author Buscaglia
36 Always, in verse

37 Spiral molecule
39 Had an effect on
40 Sudden impulse
44 Lower oneself
46 Eric B. & __ (rap group)
47 Still in it
48 Ear feature
50 Bowl yell
51 Fancy flapjack
53 Conniver's quest
54 Stirred up
55 Gravity-powered vehicles
58 Trojan War fighter
61 Bit of resistance
62 Egg __ young
63 Chapel Hill sch.
64 Wedding-announcement word

28 WHERE YOU LIVE

by Cathy Millhauser

ACROSS

1 Bullring cheers
5 Winter weather
9 Something easy
14 Old Testament book
15 Bread spread
16 Sky blue
17 Prefix for social
18 Dressed
19 Broadway awards
20 Cape Canaveral structure
23 High-fashion mag
24 Slippery one
25 Family member
28 Think alike
30 Rank beginner
32 "Snow" veggie
33 Failing totally
37 "Rule Britannia" composer
39 Wee bit
40 Toad feature
41 Does mining work
46 Mr. Lombardo
47 Bring back the line
48 Fictional Jane et al.
50 Tee's preceder
51 Singer Peeples
53 Double curve
54 Beef selections
59 Richard's *Pretty Woman* costar
62 Family member
63 Word form for "thought"
64 Trimming
65 *An American Tail* characters
66 Zilch, to Zapata
67 Bagpipers' wear
68 Fits to __
69 Frenzied

DOWN

1 Evangelist Roberts
2 Moon goddess
3 Caesar said it
4 Black eye
5 Inner-ear part
6 North's nickname
7 Low in fat
8 Sly trick
9 Library fixture
10 Arrow rival
11 Convent dweller
12 Hue's partner
13 Gentlemen
21 Music marking
22 Colony founder
25 Farm storage
26 Mythical flier
27 Rosalynn followed her
28 Hawks' homes
29 Sacred river
31 Ex-GI org.
32 National Leaguer
34 USPS delivery
35 Fall behind
36 Wedding words
38 Immigrant's course: Abbr.
42 Furniture ornaments
43 Getting __ years
44 Bequest receiver
45 Fabric worker
49 Eye feature
52 *Battlestar Galactica* commander
53 Prevention unit
54 Dagger handle
55 Cut it out
56 Gouda alternative
57 Make over
58 Become drenched
59 NYC airport
60 Mentalist Geller
61 __ Abner

29 SMART QUOTE

by Wayne R. Williams

ACROSS

1 Painter Edgar
6 Kodak spokesperson
11 Geom. shape
14 Antilles isle
15 Jacques, for one
16 She-bear: Sp.
17 START OF A QUOTE
19 Go bad
20 Minimal
21 Treats seawater
23 Odds' colleagues
24 Folklore beasts
27 Mexican city
28 Shingle letters
29 Defense org.
30 Ski spot
31 Fictional exile
32 Calls
33 MIDDLE OF QUOTE
36 Source of quote
37 Inner disposition
38 Societal standards
39 Steamed
40 Writer Sinclair
41 CO clock setting
44 Lunar plain
45 Well-behaved kid
46 Washed-out
47 Profession of 36 Across
49 Cartoonist's need
51 __ Aviv
52 END OF QUOTE
55 Dir. opp. WSW
56 Boredom
57 Biko of South Africa
58 Draft letters
59 Musical notation
60 All in

DOWN

1 Touched lightly
2 Short trip of a sort
3 Some hoopsters
4 __ *Irish Rose*
5 __ serif
6 Wall St. analyst's designation
7 Bobby of hockey
8 Like some rolls
9 Highland hillsides
10 Cravings
11 Brando Oscar role
12 U-235 and U-238
13 Tangled mess
18 Squealer
22 Stands for
25 Rival of Navratilova
26 Became unraveled
29 __ Dame
30 *The Rookie* star
31 "It" is this
32 Released, in a way
33 Brings to life
34 Crusaders' adversaries
35 Makes jump
36 Wee speck
38 Auto stat.
40 Never praised
41 Kitchen tool
42 Record holder
43 Designated
45 Unanimously
46 Singer LaBelle
48 Spud's buds
50 Be idle
53 Destructive one
54 CX

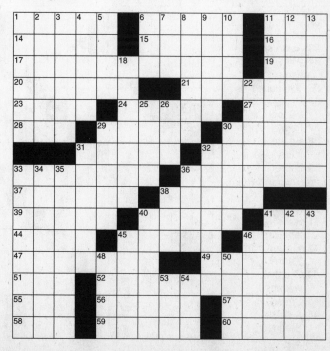

30 THUMB-THING ELSE

by Trip Payne

ACROSS

1 *West Side Story* heroine
6 Skater Thomas
10 "__ she blows!"
14 Man from Muscat
15 Author Hunter
16 Make angry
17 Thumb user
19 __ impasse
20 Supplement, with "out"
21 Frozen rain
22 Draw forth
24 Washington paper
25 Sea foam
26 Wheedle
29 Japanese vehicle
32 Clear the board
33 Asian capital
34 "What's __ name?"
35 Two cubes
36 Reservation symbol
37 Peel an apple
38 Be the interviewer
39 Lauren of *The Love Boat*
40 Birds in formation
41 Fixed leftovers
43 Viewed with alarm
44 Skunks' weapons
45 Smidgens
46 Actress Berenson
48 Arp's genre
49 By way of
52 "__ It Romantic?"
53 Thumb users
56 *Cosby Show* son
57 Flow slowly
58 Actor Lew
59 Geog. region
60 Poor grades
61 Baker's ingredient

DOWN

1 *Utopia* author
2 One way to run
3 Uncontrolled anger
4 Chemical ending
5 Pet-carrier need
6 Accounting entry
7 Mr. Knievel
8 Keep out
9 Room-to-room device
10 Characteristics
11 Thumb user
12 Jai __
13 Dollars for quarters
18 Lessen the load
23 Mischievous god
24 Prepare to be shot
25 Court assessments
26 Fragrant wood
27 Come to mind
28 Thumb user
29 Put a value on
30 Licorice flavor
31 Went down
33 Gordie and Elias
36 Frog or cat, e.g.
37 Black and Baltic
39 New Mexico art colony
40 Vacation motive
42 Journal boss
43 Cliched dog moniker
45 Toyland visitors
46 Catcher's gear
47 Laver contemporary
48 Catch some Z's
49 Actress Miles
50 Makes furious
51 Helper: Abbr.
54 Caviar
55 Caustic solution

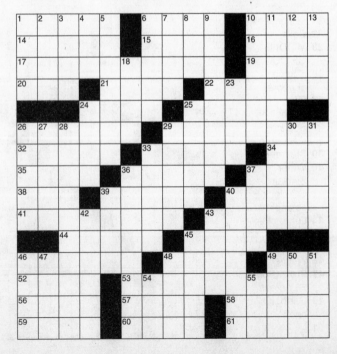

31 DANCE BAND

ACROSS

1 __ Aires
7 "Hey you!"
11 Pa Clampett
14 Tie score
15 Mustang, but not stallion
16 Poker "bullet"
17 Dancing animator?
19 __ de mer
20 Much-loved
21 Final course
23 Purina rival
26 Diet-food phrase
28 Movie pooch
29 Davis of *Thelma & Louise*
31 Thumbs-down vote
32 Wallace and Douglas
33 Witness
35 Second Beatles film
36 AAA suggestion
37 Candy-bar ingredient
39 Man-mouse link
42 Farmer's friend
44 Flower parts
46 Thumper's friend
48 Put a top on
49 Adidas alternatives
50 Nobelist Wiesel
51 Sherlock portrayer
53 Early cartoonist
54 Night light
56 Hideaway
58 Baton Rouge sch.

59 Dancing pollster?
64 __ out a living
65 Rubberneck
66 Tennis great Pancho
67 Watched Junior
68 "The __ the limit!"
69 Folksinger Pete

DOWN

1 Gift feature
2 Actress Merkel
3 Sushi selection
4 Still in progress
5 Eleven: Fr.
6 Family car
7 __ de deux
8 When *60 Minutes* is on
9 Cutlery metal
10 Stocking stuffers
11 Dancing president?
12 Two-handed card game
13 River features
18 Press corps member?
22 Go to sea
23 Ice-cream ingredient
24 Riga resident
25 Dancing colonist?
27 South American capital
30 Computer-data format
32 Breakfast fruit
34 Make leather

35 Leave __ to Heaven
38 Down in the dumps
40 Comedienne Charlotte et al.
41 Coll. prof. rank
43 Help do wrong
45 Connection
46 __-lettres
47 "Seward's Folly"
48 Storefront feature
51 Referee's order
52 Windblown soil
55 Coop group
57 Curved molding
60 Scale notes
61 Big galoot
62 Vein contents
63 Something to shoot for

32 INJECTING HUMOR

by Donna J. Stone

ACROSS

1 Lays down the lawn
5 Godunov or Badenov
10 Bassoon kin
14 Throw in the towel
15 On the ball
16 Nice or Newark
17 *The __ Reader* (literary mag)
18 Trooper's tool
19 Auel heroine
20 START OF A QUIP
23 Fathered a foal
24 "__ the Walrus" (Beatles tune)
25 Graduation gear
27 Alts.
28 Swig like a pig
32 Shogun costume
34 Missionary, often
36 Boot out
37 MIDDLE OF QUIP
40 Sailed through
42 Author Smollett
43 Copier supplies
46 Prepare to fly
47 Cover-girl Carol
50 Speedometer abbr.
51 __ jiffy
53 Metal fabrics
55 END OF QUIP
60 Saltwater fish
61 Ryan or Tatum
62 Baltic resident
63 El __, TX
64 Michelangelo masterpiece
65 Heron relative
66 "__ o'clock scholar"
67 Land on the Red Sea
68 Bound bundle

DOWN

1 Wet-sneaker sound
2 Wearing apparel
3 Bistro patrons
4 Canyon of fame
5 Roseanne Arnold, née __
6 Oil of __
7 Overhaul
8 OPEC representative
9 Make tracks
10 Whitish gem
11 Eagle, for one
12 Joan of Arc site
13 SFO stat
21 Adds fringe to
22 Brit. record label
26 Florist's need
29 Dos Passos trilogy
30 Actress Lorna
31 Spec episode
33 Brahman bellows
34 Oriental-art material
35 Marching-band member
37 Egg plant?
38 Pack complement
39 __ Selassie
40 S&L convenience
41 Mimic
44 Free (of)
45 A bit too curious
47 It multiplies by dividing
48 Soup ingredient
49 Fearsome fly
52 *Oklahoma!*'s Ado __
54 Off-the-cuff
56 Knowledgeable about
57 Be abundant
58 Hoopster Archibald
59 Pizzazz
60 Exercise place

33 HUMAN ANIMALS

by Shirley Soloway

ACROSS

1 Western wear
6 Line of poetry
11 Increases
14 Troy lady
15 Artist Matisse
16 Society-page word
17 Overachiever
19 Newsman Rather
20 Small songbird
21 Billboard displays
22 Walk out on
24 Fountain in Rome
26 More prudent
27 Edith, to Archie
30 *I Dream of Jeannie* star
33 Gee's preceder
36 Burmese or Bornean
37 Make a hole __
38 Part of RFD
40 US summer setting
41 Canceled projects
42 Up for __ (available)
43 Standing tall
45 Orly lander, once
46 Mixed bag
47 Highway menace
49 *Max __ Returns* ('83 film)
51 Blue ribbon, e.g.
54 Whirlpool rival
56 Supply troops to

58 Extra
60 Circle segment
61 WWII aviator
64 Recipe phrase
65 Hard to see
66 Lend __ (listen)
67 Drunkard
68 Bandleader Skinnay
69 Hair jobs

DOWN

1 __ out (discipline)
2 *Damn Yankees* tune
3 Inspirational author
4 Hammered, in a way
5 SAT taker
6 Backyard building
7 Afternoon socials
8 Bill to pay: Abbr.
9 Attribution
10 Brings on board
11 Nonfavored ones
12 Nectar source
13 Conveyed
18 Barbara and Conrad
23 "__ evil, hear . . ."
25 Perfume bottles
26 Poster word
28 Biblical judge
29 Port of Iraq
31 Hazzard deputy

32 Robin's roost
33 As a result
34 Roll up
35 Timid soul
37 Being dragged
39 More or less
44 Tennis pro Michael
47 Sleeve style
48 Mischievous girl
50 Faux pas
52 Reviewer Ebert
53 Wild fancy
54 *Serpico* author
55 Mr. Guthrie
56 Skirt length
57 Farm animals
59 Goes awry
62 Chinese principle
63 Dance genre

34 REVERSE ENDINGS

by Wayne R. Williams

ACROSS

1 Tip
5 Circle fully
11 Actress Gardner
14 Software buyer
15 Carolina river
16 Super __ (Lee Trevino)
17 Crooked heath?
19 "Black gold"
20 Rocking-chair locales
21 Patch a wall
23 Quite perceptive
24 Compass pt.
25 Life preserver?
33 Sour-cream product
36 Author Anita
37 Wed in haste
38 Time to remember
39 Wearing a cloak
41 Use the microwave
42 Light wood
44 Oblique line: Abbr.
45 Chicago trains
46 Where grouches worship?
50 Word after want
51 Battle of the __
55 Small generator
59 Barrymore and Richie
61 Tuscaloosa's loc.
62 Slots jackpot?
64 Forceful stream
65 Barrymore and Merman
66 Concerning
67 Woodsman's need
68 Usher again
69 Some votes

DOWN

1 *Mea* __
2 Part of PGA
3 Indian statesman
4 Land areas
5 Dueling sword
6 Beatty et al.
7 Precious stone
8 Wedding vows
9 Start up again
10 Moonstruck
11 Run __ (lose control)
12 Bridal wear
13 Wheel shaft
18 Close-call comment
22 Amoeba, for one
26 Stevedores' grp.
27 __ *Cane* ('63 film)
28 Dominant idea
29 Shiite's belief
30 Percolate
31 Milky mineral
32 __ up (livens)
33 Something owed
34 "Dies __"
35 Tropical tree
39 Landlubber's woe
40 Psyche part
43 C-__ (cable channel)
47 House and grounds
48 Band member
49 Shorebird
52 Mrs. Helmsley
53 "Battle Hymn" word
54 Senator Kefauver
55 Goya subject
56 *Family Ties* role
57 Entryway
58 Protest-singer Phil
59 Actress Kedrova
60 *Meet Me* __ *Louis*
63 Haw preceder

COMPOSITION

by Eric Albert

ACROSS

1 Neon, e.g.
8 Avoided the issue
15 Bring up
16 Part at the start
17 START OF A ROSSINI QUOTE
18 Free
19 Handle badly
20 Sounded the horn
21 Falsification
22 I is one
27 Feminine ending
28 PART 2 OF QUOTE
33 Regarded with reverence
34 New York county
35 New York county
38 Gas rating
40 High-school outcast
41 Hardly touch
44 PART 3 OF QUOTE
47 Doctor's charge
50 Got too big for
51 Rule, in India
52 Donnybrook
56 Too big
58 Rice dish
60 END OF QUOTE
62 Nickname of a sort
63 Police ploy
64 Last course
65 Detection devices

DOWN

1 Provide a feast for
2 Outs
3 Casino shows
4 Nights before
5 Careful strategy
6 Munched on
7 Vast expanse
8 FDR program
9 Dudley Moore film
10 Major crime
11 Kind of custard
12 Wait in the shadows
13 Competitive advantage
14 Action
23 Off-color
24 __ Town
25 Vane reading
26 Off-the-wall
29 Riga resident
30 Keogh alternative
31 Beelzebub's business
32 Ball holder
33 Literary alias
35 __ Khan
36 Author Deighton
37 Garden spot
38 "__ from Muskogee"
39 Pfeiffer role
41 S.F. setting
42 Line of thought?: Abbr.
43 Mid.
45 Can't stand
46 Hair quality
47 Raisin center
48 Less trouble
49 Tosses out
52 Ginger's partner
53 Perfect for picking
54 Warts and all
55 Folding beds
57 Elmer's nemesis
59 Mel of Cooperstown
60 6-pt. scores
61 Mine rocks

36 GROUNDKEEPERS

by Wayne R. Williams

ACROSS

1 Health resort
4 Hotshot
7 Kind of camera: Abbr.
10 Singer Stafford et al.
13 Steam engine
15 DMV procedure
17 Set up
18 Thankless one
19 Chopin's *chérie*
21 Blood quantity
22 Stitched
23 Teachers' org.
24 Latin 101 verb
25 Hindu mystics
29 Genetic letters
30 Shade source
33 Came to earth
34 Sell out
37 Bossy's comment
38 *Aida* guy
40 That girl
41 Throbs
43 Irrigation need
44 Calls one's own
45 Bandleader Brown
46 Short snooze
48 Forks over
50 Tammy Faye's former grp.
51 Take off
55 Novelist Seton
56 *Steel Magnolias* star
60 Speak hesitatingly
62 Too old
63 Saved, as a mag article
64 Old pro
65 Partnership word
66 Paid notices
67 Compass dir.
68 Mos. and mos.

DOWN

1 Some deer
2 Blender setting
3 Hood's missile
4 Building add-on
5 *Picnic* playwright
6 Ultimate letters
7 Fishing nets
8 Actress Carter
9 Rule: Abbr.
10 *Upstairs, Downstairs* star
11 Caesar's port
12 Doesn't dele
14 Hayloft locales
16 Hooky player
20 Testifier of '91
26 Merchandise
27 "Woe is me!"
28 Ctr.
29 Bowler's button
30 Nero, for one: Abbr.
31 Bud's partner
32 Famous feminist
34 Mrs. Truman
35 Light-dawning cry
36 "Absolutely!"
39 Shemp's brother
42 Turkish staple
46 Is taken aback
47 Burning
48 Rigatoni, e.g.
49 Singer Susan
50 Alias: Abbr.
52 Psychedelic doctor
53 *Pomp and Circumstance* composer
54 Idyllic places
57 Tennis term
58 Actor Montand
59 Honor with a party
61 Extinct bird

37 BODY BEATERS

by Randolph Ross

ACROSS

1 Dieter's entree
6 Ran into
9 Fitting
12 Handsome guy
14 Home to billions
16 Bowl sound
17 Rousing hoedown tune
19 LP filler
20 Sixth sense
21 Tough puzzle
23 Laissez-__
24 "Life Is Just __ of Cherries"
25 Terrestrial
28 Middle Easterner
29 Comet and friends
32 Salinger girl
35 Current unit
36 Took a rip (at)
38 *Shop __ You Drop*
39 Disoriented
41 Side dishes
44 Chagall and Antony
47 Code of silence
48 Craze
49 One of the Chipmunks
51 Unfaithful friend
53 Vane dir.
56 Lodge member
57 Funny joke
59 Pub choice
60 Royal address
61 Second banana
62 *Mal de __*
63 Poker pile
64 John of rock

DOWN

1 Out of danger
2 Fusses
3 Airplane maneuver
4 Hill builder
5 Break up
6 Ike's missus
7 Sports Channel rival
8 Clasp of a sort
9 Threatening one
10 Expert group
11 Hammer wielder
13 Long steps
15 Isle off Venezuela
18 Boathouse hanging
22 Unit of sound
23 Summer appliance
25 Like Sabin's vaccine
26 Verne character
27 Tasty morsel
28 "Small world, __ it?"
30 Mas that baa
31 Winning streak
33 Oven accessory
34 Designer Schiaparelli
37 Kowtows
40 Scuba gear
42 Bahrain, for one
43 *Tin __* ('87 film)
45 Takes a chance
46 Siamese attraction
48 *Atlantic City* director
49 Red as __
50 Butcher's wts.
51 Smile broadly
52 Space starter
53 Dalmatian's name
54 Utah state flower
55 British architect
58 Campaign pro

38 MONSTROUS

by Trip Payne

ACROSS

1 Vinegar acid
7 On the __ (fleeing)
10 Eye part
14 Texas city
15 College climber
16 Hockey player's protection
17 European airline
18 Make known
19 Tavern buys
20 Monster you can't fool?
23 Become one
26 Part of TNT
27 Squeaker or squealer
28 High transport
29 Dodger Hershiser
31 Ethereal
33 Church areas
35 Smart aleck
37 Tiny, to Burns
38 Monster's game equipment?
42 __ in "nudnik"
43 Raymond Burr role
45 Dull hues
48 __ uproar
49 Work hard
50 Tiriac of tennis
51 "__ your old man!"
53 Crumpet complement
55 Napoleonic marshal
56 Monstrous novel?
60 Melville opus
61 __ *Kapital*
62 Wild equine
66 Become winded
67 Sign a contract
68 Soda units
69 Red and Black
70 Both Begleys
71 Go AWOL

DOWN

1 Ms. MacGraw
2 Bandleader Calloway
3 Prior to, in poetry
4 Period of office
5 Dostoyevsky character
6 Where to park your parkas
7 Taleteller
8 Oversized birdcage
9 *The Thin Man* name
10 __ the crack of dawn
11 Holds dear
12 Channel swimmer
13 Determine worth
21 "Sacred" word form
22 Cossack leader
23 "That's super!"
24 Actor Estrada
25 Lucie's dad
30 Comedian Bruce
32 Kidney enzyme
34 Coors rival
36 '92 Wimbledon winner
37 Absolutely
39 *Persona non* __
40 Zodiac beast
41 McClurg of movies
44 Bridge expert Culbertson
45 Legs of lamb
46 Dormmate
47 Mother on *Bewitched*
48 Bali, but not Mali
52 Goody, maybe
54 Palmer, to pals
57 Caldwell et al.
58 Suggests a price
59 Scarfs down
63 "__ whillikers!"
64 Make a miscue
65 Q-U connectors

39 SOMETHING'S BREWING

ACROSS

1 A Leno predecessor
5 Picket-line crosser
9 Beef-rating org.
13 Cartoonist Peter
14 There's nothing in it
15 Stuck-up person
16 Reviewer Rex
17 Essayist's alias
18 Practice piece
19 Voice of the teapot in *Beauty and the Beast*
22 Rabbit-sized rodent
23 Publicize loudly
24 Carroll's teapot dweller
29 Buffalo NHLers
33 Overwhelming emotion
34 Gene carriers
35 Van Gogh locale
36 Author Rand
37 Assail
38 WWII contingent
39 I love, to Livy
40 Travel-guide name
41 Teapot Dome figure
44 Freight hauler
45 Utter bomb
49 Tempest in a teapot
53 Two-time Nobelist
54 Assemble a film
55 Caron film
56 Fort Knox bar
57 Dinner bed, often
58 Made a misstatement
59 Former South Yemen capital
60 Spree
61 Foal's father

DOWN

1 Graph lead-in
2 Field of battle
3 "Wall Street Lays __"
4 Copland opus
5 Knife cases
6 Lassie, e.g.
7 *Inter* __ (among other things)
8 Boston's nickname
9 Not schooled
10 Like lime pie
11 Comedian Goodman
12 Feasted on
15 Organic lubricant
20 Guitars' ancestors
21 Miffed
25 *The __ the Jackal*
26 Golden Rule word
27 European valley
28 Guesses: Abbr.
29 "I never __ purple cow"
30 Asian sea
31 Tell all
32 Economic downturn
36 Sometimes-shy person
37 Kind of eclipse
39 Word form for "air"
40 Move to and fro quickly
42 Bowl-O-Rama button
43 Somalia's home
46 Operadom's "Bubbles"
47 IV x XXVII
48 Cargo ship
49 It may be mutual
50 Exhort
51 Singer Adams
52 __-de-camp
53 Espionage grp.

TIMELY ADVICE

by Donna J. Stone

ACROSS

1 Coral and Red
5 Discombobulate
10 Church area
14 David's instrument
15 Producer Ponti
16 Thailand neighbor
17 As a result
18 Right: Fr.
19 "__ forgive those . . ."
20 START OF A QUIP
23 Soothes
24 Junior, for one
25 '20s auto
28 Fish-and-chips partner
29 "If I __ Hammer"
33 Telescope view
35 Hairdresser's nightmare
37 Pianist Gilels
38 MIDDLE OF QUIP
42 Jupiter's alias
43 Watering hole
44 Jittery
47 Be important
48 Supermarket-scanner data: Abbr.
51 Teut.
52 Baseball great Mel
54 Dogpatch dweller
56 END OF QUIP
61 It's nothing
63 Coleco competitor
64 Blue hue
65 Eternally
66 __ so many words

67 Wear a long face
68 Florida county
69 Pass a law
70 Sound-stage areas

DOWN

1 Aussie woman
2 Sharp scolding
3 Sock style
4 Spinning-reel part
5 Electrically versatile
6 Theda of the silents
7 Elvis __ Presley
8 Opens an envelope
9 Frank
10 Jai __
11 Deli delicacy
12 Piglet's mom
13 Vane dir.
21 Leading man?
22 Strangers __ Train
26 Leave the stage
27 Thimble Theater name
30 Citrus cooler
31 Air conduit
32 __ Is Born
34 Boxer Spinks
35 TV talker
36 Peace Nobelist Myrdal
38 Lane marker
39 Like some nobility
40 Even so

41 Sheer fear
42 Run for the health of it
45 Came by
46 Natural gas component
48 Inimitable
49 Next-to-last syllable
50 Haunted-house sounds
53 Rocky Mountain range
55 Bill of fashion
57 Knight time
58 Bank deposit?
59 Author Ambler
60 "__ She Sweet?"
61 Last letter in the OED
62 Zsa Zsa's sister

41 STRANGE QUARTERS

by Randolph Ross

ACROSS

1 Havana honcho
7 Tennis pro, often
14 Wind instrument
16 Take a rest
17 Defensive wall
18 Stockpiles
19 Rock stars, to teens
20 *Bolero* composer
22 *Pinta* partner
23 Tiny touches
24 "__ 'em!" (coach's exhortation)
29 Bit of comedy
30 Make repairs to
31 Lead astray
32 Efficiency apartment?
34 High-rise fortune teller?
35 Deluxe aerie?
37 Sandinista leader
38 Some sisters
39 Blushing
42 Rear parts, in anatomy
43 Reagan Secretary of State
44 "__ Ha'i"
45 Shed, in Sheffield
47 Stalagmite fan
48 Winery activity
52 Hard to catch
54 Rashly
55 Troop group
56 Loud speaker
57 Fairly good

DOWN

1 Managing somehow
2 Maine national park
3 Lamour costume
4 Song refrain
5 They'll be darned
6 "Let Me Be the __"
7 Eastern Europeans
8 Precious resource
9 Val Kilmer film of '85
10 "__ bodkins!"
11 Ring stats
12 Lea lady
13 TLC dispensers
15 Willy-nilly
21 In the gut
23 Neural branches
25 Hatred
26 Judy Garland, née __
27 Old French coin
28 President pro __
30 No philanderer
31 It may be on the house
32 Secret messages
33 Soup or salad
34 It holds a qt. of milk
35 *The Bride Came* __
36 Coronado's quest
39 Deep ditch
40 News time
41 Worst-case descriptor
43 More immense
44 Fundamental
46 Aware of
47 Medical discovery
48 "__ the season . . ."
49 Hill builder
50 That girl
51 Summer shade
53 Youngster

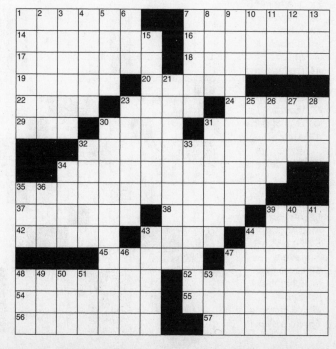

42 CITRUS MUSIC

by Cathy Millhauser

ACROSS

1 Make an exchange
5 Mardi __
9 Bette, in *All About Eve*
14 Prepare __ (the way)
15 Roof runoff
16 Nautical adverb
17 Son of Zeus
18 Dismantle
19 Potter's finish
20 Citric Dylan tune?
23 Mighty peculiar
24 Three, in Capri
25 Goat quote
28 Court cry
31 In
36 Creator of Boy
38 Keep at it
40 Alamo rival
41 Citric Welk group?
44 Reagan and Howard
45 Like Nash's lama
46 Half of deca-
47 Armed swimmers
49 Wonderland bird
51 Averse to mingling
52 African slitherer
54 Rap-sheet letters
56 Citric Glen Campbell tune?
64 All over
65 Be a kvetch
66 Revolution line
68 Word expert Peter Mark __
69 Musical tempo
70 Greek philosopher
71 Make an LP
72 Preeminent
73 Churchill's successor

DOWN

1 Springs are here
2 Nice and friendly
3 State confidently
4 Green sauce
5 Solomon of rhyme
6 Called up
7 Go-fer
8 Quick drink
9 Fridge device
10 *M*A*S*H* nurse
11 Stationery stack
12 Mideast region
13 Soothsayer's sign
21 Find smashing
22 Qum resident
25 Part of MGM
26 Literally, "for this"
27 Catalyst, e.g.
29 Mr. von Furstenberg
30 Marked off, in a way
32 Find awful
33 Bakery hardware
34 Jolly feeling
35 Opinion piece
37 To boot
39 Peace Prize city
42 Humid
43 Piped up
48 Palette set
50 Flue feature
53 Warsaw et al.
55 Make gape
56 Distort
57 Inventor Sikorsky
58 Hockey structure
59 Goes quickly
60 French milk
61 __ *La Douce*
62 Cut down
63 Mid evening
67 Chip off the old block

43 MONETARY POLICY

by Eric Albert

ACROSS

1 Jezebel's husband
5 Disconcert
10 *Ghost* cast name
14 Lose appeal
15 He-manly
16 Beasts of burden
17 Birthright barterer
18 Dampen with drops
19 __ Hari
20 START OF A QUIP
23 Key of one flat
25 Wedding walkway
26 Of a sense
27 Summon silently
31 Black as night
32 *The Third Man* actor
33 Class-rank stat.
36 Baseball great Speaker
37 MIDDLE OF QUIP
38 Biceps exercise
39 Darling
40 Catch in a lie
41 Frozen raindrops
42 Made a quick note
43 Ms. Gaynor
44 Yellowish brown
47 Bad temper
48 END OF QUIP
53 Spread in a tub
54 Oil source
55 Be stunning
58 Founding father?
59 Ward off
60 First name in fashion
61 Sandbox patron
62 Put to use
63 Criminal crowd

DOWN

1 *The Naked* __
2 Is owner of
3 *Freebie and the Bean* star
4 Toronto team
5 Fossil resin
6 Boxer Max
7 Aussie rock group
8 New York ballpark
9 Bay
10 Field of activity
11 Checkups, for example
12 Oxide component
13 Foolish
21 Encyclopedia bk.
22 Myanmar neighbor
23 Orchestra leader Percy
24 Saki's real name
27 Suit
28 Marry in haste
29 Make murky
30 Iodine source
32 Toad feature
33 OAS member
34 Hold dear
35 Dead tired
38 Sidewalk vendor's offering
40 Corrida cry
42 Robbins of Broadway
43 Speed-limit letters
44 WWII craft
45 Antiquated
46 Piece of luck
47 Refine ore
49 Was dressed in
50 Bend an elbow
51 Pickable
52 Recovered from
56 Buddhist belief
57 Silly Putty holder

44 IN THE MOOD

by Randolph Ross

ACROSS

1 Rummy variety
8 Seed coverings
13 Fellow employee
14 They have brains
15 Cooperating in crime
16 "__ Mountain High Enough"
17 Kennedy matriarch
18 Dali feature
20 Binge
21 Half the world
22 __ *Championship Season*
25 Pitcher feature
28 Seventh-century date
30 Cosmic countenance
35 Judge's shout
36 Spiteful ones
37 Expected
38 Match a raise
39 Informal refusals
40 Gov't purchasing org.
42 Reference-book name
46 Congealment
49 Normandy town
53 "Amen!"
54 Rational thinker
56 "¡__ días!"

57 May birthstones
58 Rose oil
59 Saw again

DOWN

1 Michigan arena
2 Inspires grandly
3 Bit of marginalia
4 Mr. Carney
5 Economize
6 Sax range
7 State one's case
8 Met highlight
9 Southfork, e.g.
10 Wealthy
11 Ball-game summaries

12 __ Paulo, Brazil
13 Sleeper, for one
14 Garfield, but not Roosevelt
19 Stew
20 *A __ Born*
22 Completely
23 Limits risk
24 Home of Iowa State
26 "Excuse me!"
27 Eat one's words
29 Kind of verb: Abbr.
30 Mike or Mary
31 Half the course
32 Trainee

33 Unspecified degree
34 "__ Lisa"
41 Field of battle
43 Texas tackler
44 Folklore being
45 __ on (urged)
47 Big name in fashion
48 UFO crew
49 "Get lost!"
50 Bathroom square
51 *Shane* star
52 Switch settings
53 Entrepreneur's agcy.
55 S&L offering

45 PLAY BALL!

by Eric Albert

ACROSS

1 Indonesian island
5 Decision-making power
10 Finn's floater
14 __ vincit omnia
15 Body of soldiers
16 Gardner of mystery
17 Kids' game
20 Compass pt.
21 Sills solo
22 Pick up on
23 Mötley __ (rock group)
24 Fischer's opponent
25 Pack up and leave
28 On __ with (equal to)
29 Blue as the sky
30 Close-fitting
31 Mess-hall meal
35 Woody Allen, in *Bananas*
38 Fuss
39 River Napoleon navigated
40 Par minus two
41 Stare slack-jawed
42 *Mr. Ed* is one
43 Take a wrong turn
47 Renders speechless
48 Assert without proof
49 "Oh!"
50 "Mamma" follower
53 Deteriorating
56 State strongly
57 Full
58 Singer Fitzgerald
59 Sleuth Wolfe
60 Dark hardwood
61 Become lachrymose

DOWN

1 Make fun of
2 Author Kingsley
3 Cast a ballot
4 Circle segment
5 Foment
6 *L.A. Law* lawyer
7 Exercise system
8 Soak (up)
9 Where columns are found
10 Landlord's loot
11 First sign
12 Small bit
13 Easily irritated
18 Did damage to
19 Not far off
23 Composer Gian __ Menotti
24 White of a wave
25 Plumb loco
26 Singer Pinza
27 Signaled an anchor
28 Point of view
30 Cuts quickly
31 Course meeting
32 Lofty
33 Scandinavian city
34 Sigh of relief
36 Kind of
37 River embankments
41 Chevalier musical
42 Like a suit fabric
43 Cartoonist Wilson
44 Martini garnish
45 Make a change
46 Part of MGM
47 Very pale
49 "Take __ the Limit"
50 Track distance
51 Wait at a light
52 Without delay: Abbr.
54 Chew the fat
55 Royal Botanic Gardens site

46 SHELL SHOCK

by Fred Piscop

ACROSS

1 Boxer Max
5 __ to stern
9 Teases
14 Choir member
15 "__ a heart!"
16 Exemplar of perfection
17 Police, slangily
18 Cheater's sleeveful
19 Montreal's subway
20 Newscaster on the half shell?
23 Spot to drive from
24 Long. crosser
25 Lubricate anew
28 Animal-product eschewer
31 *The __ and I*
34 Petroleum giant
35 __-pop (family-owned)
36 Mr. Onassis
37 Trapper on the half shell?
40 Summer drink
41 Overjoys
42 Banana throwaway
43 "And I Love __" (Beatles tune)
44 Tom Jones' birthplace
45 Finches and pheasants
46 Make a dress
47 Wag's wordplay
48 Actress on the half shell?
55 Food-processor setting
56 Sullen
57 Oolong and pekoe
59 Less cordial
60 Lively subjects
61 Admiral Zumwalt
62 Pains in the neck
63 Chess ending
64 Bread and booze

DOWN

1 Word from Scrooge
2 Actor Baldwin
3 Latin list ender
4 Earth's action
5 *Evening __* (sitcom)
6 Sonora snack
7 Neck and neck
8 Arizona city
9 Excellent
10 What "i.e." stands for
11 Turn down
12 Have coming
13 __-mo replay
21 Blanc or Tillis
22 Grassy plains
25 Indian chief
26 Wear away
27 Earthy color
28 Soundtrack component
29 Overact
30 Comic Kaplan's namesakes
31 Buffet patron
32 Conquistador's quality
33 Half the third-graders
35 African nation
38 Ring bearers
39 She never married
45 Kramden's vehicle
46 Sloppy precipitation
47 Prize money
48 *Time* founder
49 Crocus kin
50 __ *Bede* (Eliot novel)
51 Vaudevillian Bayes
52 Jeff's partner
53 Slippery
54 Like some excuses
55 Dickens character
58 Sea plea

47 HOLD THAT TIGER

by Trip Payne

ACROSS

1 Trick takers, often
5 Moves diagonally
9 Where to detrain
14 With the exception of
15 *Mirabella* rival
16 Kind of football
17 No contest, e.g.
18 Circus musician
19 Stuck in the mud
20 Cereal with a tiger mascot
23 Vaudevillian Eddie
24 __ up (be honest)
25 Play for time
28 Go nuts, with "out"
30 Circumference segment
33 Indulging in revelry
34 Roger of *Cheers*
35 *Jacta __ est*
36 Comic strip with a tiger
39 Swiss artist
40 Screenwriter James
41 Computer accessory
42 In the dumps
43 Crop pest
44 Stocked with weapons
45 Cook book
46 Corn or form starter
47 Description of Blake's tiger
53 Perry destination
54 Rocky spot
55 New York college
57 Without company
58 __ *Kleine Nachtmusik*
59 Any thing at all
60 *The Maids* playwright
61 Zipped along
62 Singer James

DOWN

1 Little viper
2 Barn baby
3 For all time
4 Pacino film
5 Like some sauces
6 Nautical adverb
7 Pleased as punch
8 Livestock device
9 Linen fabric
10 Satie and Estrada
11 *Fils'* parent
12 *The Defiant __*
13 Lincoln son
21 Conductor Georg
22 Pet-shop purchase
25 Loots
26 Refrain sounds
27 Was under the weather
28 Room fresheners
29 Richards of tennis
30 Obsolete platter
31 Singer Della
32 Scoped out
35 Goolagong is one
37 Wynonna's mother
38 Muscat fellow
43 Easter finery
45 Poet Hart
46 Egged on
47 Loft cube
48 Fairy-tale word
49 Film worker
50 Poison
51 A lot of fun
52 Cross-shaped fastener
53 Wild tear
56 Airline to Tokyo

48 HORSING AROUND

by Karen Hodge

ACROSS

1 Bit of barbecue
4 Author Ferber
8 Carpenter's tool
13 Just standing around
15 Former sr.
16 Take __ (throw the bout)
17 Colt's stable?
19 Carnation containers
20 Beast of Borden
21 Nag's sickness?
23 Attack
25 Bowling surface
26 Ski-resort machine
28 Distinct styles
33 Sound sheepish
36 Hairdo
39 *My Three Sons* role
40 Newlywed horses' dream?
44 Take care of
45 Asian fruits
46 Q-U link
47 Fords of the '50s
49 Sewer line?
52 Seep slowly
55 Con jobs
58 Equine charm?
63 Captures on paper
65 Neighborhoods
66 Mustang menagerie?
68 Oscar de la __
69 Assigned function
70 Admired one

71 Alpine strain
72 Jean Auel character
73 Be a landlord

DOWN

1 Swarming (with)
2 Admired ones
3 Great time
4 Freud's concern
5 Tap one's fingers
6 Kind of congestion
7 Author Rogers St. Johns
8 Pale purple
9 Wax-covered cheese
10 Passport stamp
11 At any time
12 __ majesty (high crime)
14 Mr. Ness
18 Dagwood's neighbor
22 Police-blotter abbr.
24 Nutmeg spice
27 It's over your head
29 Like some vbs.
30 __ about
31 Farrow et al.
32 Shipped off
33 Army outpost
34 Imitated
35 Potent potables
37 "__ Were a Rich Man"
38 Confused states
41 Polished off

42 Movie-hype word
43 Takes off the shelf
48 Soak (up)
50 Current letters
51 Wetlands
53 African equine
54 Jetson kid
56 "__ tov!"
57 Made a vow
58 Grant from Hollywood
59 Hydrox rival
60 Libraries do it
61 *Little Man __* (Foster film)
62 Take it easy
64 Flue grime
67 Teachers' org.

49 ACTING CLASS

by A.J. Santora

ACROSS
1 Women's mag
5 Overcharge
9 General Dayan
14 Witt maneuver
15 *Star Trek* propulsion
17 Betting setting
18 *Death Becomes Her* star
19 Coach Parseghian
20 Electrical units
21 Fencing sword
22 __ a dime
24 Last year's plebe
26 Real-estate abbr.
27 Smarmy to the max
29 Most unhappy
31 Works hard
32 Cashmere kin
35 Moffo of opera
36 Batter of verse
37 "__ a man with . . ."
41 Makes fun of
43 Kroft of *60 Minutes*
44 Chapter XI column
47 Gives in
49 Area code 302: Abbr.
50 Start off
53 Rogers' rope
54 Ed or Nancy of TV
56 Having troubles
58 Dernier __ (latest fashion)
59 *Thelma & Louise* star
61 Green stone
62 Poll subject of '92
63 Mars' alias
64 Percolates
65 Yale students
66 Polite bloke

DOWN
1 Ringling Brothers' home
2 Elbow grease
3 *Havana* star
4 Eb's wife
5 Cosmos' Carl et al.
6 __ close to schedule
7 US booster rocket
8 Buddy
9 Author Rita __ Brown
10 Will-__-wisp
11 Food basic
12 Ax handlers
13 Mariel's grandpa
16 Bungle
20 The enemy
23 *The Greatest Story Ever Told* role
25 __ polloi
28 Govt. agent
30 Mailer's profession
33 East, in Essen
34 "__ real nowhere man"
36 Some teeth
38 Health program
39 *Our Miss Brooks* star
40 Most peevish
42 From __ Z
43 Swindle
44 Old sayings
45 Dionysus' mother
46 Floppy-disk holder
48 Envelope attachments
51 Maternally related
52 Part of USNA
55 Cut quickly
57 Rock legend Hendrix
60 Foolish sort
61 Binge

by Randolph Ross

ACROSS

1 Uno follower
4 Scads
8 Engine cos.
11 Additional phones: Abbr.
13 Nintendo forerunner
14 Long journey
15 With *The*, Lee Marvin film of '67
17 Replete (with)
18 Australian city
19 Musical transition
20 Murphy had one
21 Buttons or Barber
22 Certain psychologist
24 ME-to-FL hwy.
25 Hero of the '54 World Series
27 Posted
29 Work on a persistent squeak
30 Hash house
35 Some carolers
36 Letter opener
39 Blues great
45 Animation frame
46 Agitated states
47 Cut (off)
48 Bear: Sp.
49 Björn Borg, e.g.
50 Fertilizer chemicals
52 Moa relative
53 Loaded
55 "The doctor __"
56 Author James et al.
57 Pre- kin
58 Hallow ending
59 Actress Diana
60 Slalom curve

DOWN

1 Joyce hero
2 Enzyme class
3 Spreading around
4 Disagreeing
5 Use a hammock
6 Vein contents
7 Badge material
8 Quite cold
9 Disarm
10 Shooting events
12 "Gateway to the West": Abbr.
13 Parting word
14 Operatic effects
16 Feminist Molly
19 Onetime Amoco rival
22 They may have it
23 De __ (too much)
26 Secret meeting
28 Redeemed
31 Family Ties mom
32 Periodic-table no.
33 In order (to)
34 $C_{10}H_{14}N_2$
37 Takes out, in a way
38 Muddles through puddles
39 Carter secretary of state
40 Not so smart
41 Attracted
42 Exclusive groups
43 David Lee and Philip
44 Like a gymnast
50 Padre or Pirate, for short
51 Southern constellation
53 Mania
54 "__ to Extremes" (Billy Joel tune)

51 TRUE GRID

by Fred Piscop

ACROSS

1 Air conduit
5 Crockett defended it
10 Are: Sp.
14 Job-safety org.
15 Sand bit
16 Time-machine destination
17 Footballer's detention center?
19 "__ first you don't . . ."
20 *The War of the Worlds* visitor
21 Make out
23 Church area
24 Grove
25 Printer's proof
28 Temple quorum
31 Where it's at
34 Melon cover
36 Answer back
37 NOW cause
38 Debate side
39 Mr. Carney
41 Native: Suffix
42 Ice-cream flavor
44 High-flying toy
46 Agitated state
47 Stamp-pad devices
49 TV option
51 Taoism founder
53 Photographer Adams
57 Harsh-tempered
59 Ninepins pin
61 Blubbers
62 Footballer's magazine photo?
64 Turkey __ (dance)

65 Prepare to be knighted
66 Cassini of fashion
67 Aussie rockers
68 Walk heavily
69 French statesman Coty

DOWN

1 Tenet
2 Run-of-the-mill
3 Visual aid
4 Steak order
5 Turkish official
6 Author Hubbard
7 Track-meet org.
8 Botch up
9 Egotistic belief
10 Unisex
11 Footballer's fastener?

12 Ivan, for one
13 Envelope abbr.
18 Grievous
22 Avoid, as an issue
24 __ voyage
26 __ bono (free)
27 Orr's milieu
29 Word form for "height"
30 Nikolai's negative
31 Trucker's wheels
32 Mashie or niblick
33 Footballer's fishing gear?
35 *Star Trek* character
38 Chocolate substitute
40 Confederate

43 Publishing family
45 Freezer product
46 Bought by mail
48 Stays on
50 Hibernation station
52 Skunk's trademark
54 Made off with
55 Novelist Glasgow
56 Narrow shelf
57 Wine region
58 Country humor
59 Watch part
60 Some seaweed
63 Classical beginning

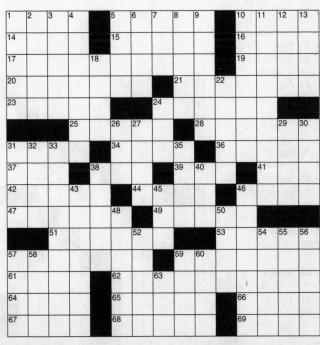

by Trip Payne

ACROSS

1 Eyeglasses, for short
6 Red-tag event
10 Blue shade
14 Marsh bird
15 Mr. Love?
16 Phoenix team
17 "What's that bird overhead, Tonto?"
19 South American monkey
20 Lots of quires
21 Romania, once
22 Retro singing group
25 Pay attention
26 *Mommie __*
27 Actor Gerard
28 '60s protest grp.
29 Forgets about
30 Brief beachwear
32 Puts on TV
33 Blackmore character
35 Joyce of *Roc*
38 Secretary's task
40 Spelunking fan
41 Part of MPH
43 Slaloming shape
44 Sign of the future
46 Baal's challenger
48 Some promgoers
49 Magi
50 Temple's trademark
51 Smokes, for short
52 "How was that joke, Gumby?"
57 Tighten __ belt
58 Supplements, with "out"
59 Pica alternative
60 Subjunctive word
61 TV's Batman
62 Stay a subscriber

DOWN

1 Get the point
2 Faldo's grp.
3 Unit of work
4 Animation art
5 Author Laurence et al.
6 Trig term
7 Bouquet
8 Gehrig and Gossett
9 Atlanta's zone: Abbr.
10 __ *Is Born*
11 "How fast should I go, Lone Ranger?"
12 Let loose
13 Mongols, e.g.
18 Half-__ over (tipsy)
21 Melting-watch painter
22 Prefix for sweet
23 "What's my mane made of, Roy?"
24 Bohemian
25 Price rise
26 Quaid film of '88
27 Juniper product
30 Cranberry spot
31 "How keen!"
33 Couch potato's dream device
34 Switch positions
36 Microscope part
37 Thou follower
39 Soup ingredient
40 Fridge section
41 Donna of *Angie*
42 Stritch or May
44 Most pristine
45 Sale-ad word
47 Senator Helms
48 Record machines
50 Royal Crown rival
52 Chop down
53 Word a matador adores
54 Relatives
55 Somme time
56 Bow wood

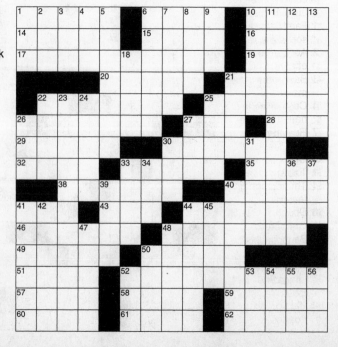

NOW HEAR THIS

by Matt Gaffney

ACROSS
1 Explorer Amundsen
6 Applies grease to
11 Some ammo
14 Telecast component
15 "Me, __ I call myself"
16 "*Certainement!*"
17 SOUND SLEEPER
20 Ms. Caldwell
21 Song refrain
22 Seep slowly
23 Larry King's network
24 Sarge's shout
27 *Taxi* star
30 Slobber
33 Glass square
34 America's Cup contender
38 LEAKY TIRE
41 Fan, sometimes
42 August Moon offerings
43 Basketball maneuver
44 Casino naturals
47 Russian refusals
50 Grill's partner
51 Tough spot
54 Thumbprint feature
56 Douglas, e.g.
59 GHOST
63 Be in the red
64 War cry
65 Apartments
66 Old crony
67 Barn adjuncts
68 Electrical device

DOWN
1 Deride
2 Moussaka washdown
3 Pickaxe relative
4 Columnist Smith
5 A whole bunch
6 Take it easy
7 WWII town
8 Gillette invention
9 Cease-fire region: Abbr.
10 "__ you!"
11 Dunderhead
12 Edwin Aldrin
13 Shoe clerk's query
18 Canadian export
19 Religion founder
23 Louder, to Liszt
25 Banned insecticides
26 Messes up
27 Cellar-door attachments
28 Cartographic closeup
29 Archaic verb
31 Merlin of TV
32 Hartman and Kirk
33 Ltr. addenda
35 *For the Boys* grp.
36 Ukr. and Lith., formerly
37 Pompous sort
39 Stick around
40 Store-window word
45 Spain's longest river
46 Grounds for the Victoria Cross
48 __ a kind (poker hand)
49 "Go ahead!"
51 Cartoon coquette
52 Tom Harkin's state
53 "The First __"
55 "Uh-oh" cousin
56 Thwart a plot
57 Tiny amount
58 Promising
60 Athena's symbol
61 "What have we here?"
62 *A Chorus Line* finale

SHIP SHAPE

by Shirley Soloway

ACROSS

1 Head over heels
5 Devonshire drinks
9 Flowers-to-be
13 Actor Richard
14 "__ we all?"
15 On a cruise
16 Incline
17 Makes wait, in a way
19 Feeling poorly
20 California county
21 High-school student
23 Modify copy
27 Ginza gelt
28 Dogpatch's Daisy __
30 "__ out? Decide!"
31 Cassette player
34 Army priests
36 *Hawaii Five-O* star
37 More cunning
39 Byron works
40 Seals' singing partner
42 Least lax
44 Guided trip
45 Retirees' org.
46 One's partner
47 On fire
49 Fashion expressions
52 Halogen salts
55 Crude cabin
56 Acknowledging applause
60 Garage job
61 Grand in scale
62 Road reversal
63 Author Wiesel
64 Love too much
65 Gives permission to
66 Iditarod vehicle

DOWN

1 See the light
2 Well-coordinated
3 Typesetter's sheet
4 Strong bug
5 Make __ for it (escape)
6 Baltic resident
7 Give guarantees
8 Put away
9 "Nonsense!"
10 Soldier-show grp.
11 DuPont's HQ
12 Down in the dumps
14 Little or Frye
18 Gymnast Comaneci
20 Some machines do it
22 Necessary
24 "My One __"
25 FDR confidant
26 Boulevard liners
28 CCXXX quintupled
29 *Prelude to __* ('92 film)
31 Close attention, for short
32 Heart line
33 Pothook shape
34 Ante- kin
35 Jet-set plane
38 Frat letter
41 Get into condition
43 "Darn it!"
45 Unruffled
48 Business bigwig
49 Created clothing
50 James Blake's nickname
51 Fine mount
53 Be adjacent to
54 Craggy hills
56 Danson of *Cheers*
57 Overseas addr.
58 Baby beaver
59 Rocks at the bar
60 Bandleader Brown

55 TOP BANANAS

by A.J. Santora

ACROSS

1 *Bells __ Ringing*
4 Actress Dalton
8 __ deux
13 Pol. party
14 Silents star
15 Market for goods
16 Rocks with rye
17 Top banana in baseball
19 Top banana in movies
21 Scale notes
22 Overwhelm
23 Dublin distances
25 Fits to __
26 Clumsy one
29 Mrs. Kovacs
31 Acts to excess
34 First woman M.P.
35 Top bananas at concerts
39 *Tugboat __*
40 Went fishing
41 Phaser setting
42 Bishop's domain
43 *Twelve O'Clock High* grp.
47 Stand __ stead
51 Bantu language
53 Religious deg.
54 What top bananas get
57 Top banana in vaudeville
59 Name in UN history
60 Shaw et al.
61 Slightly open
62 Brittany season
63 "__ is human"
64 Singing syllables
65 Bolshevik

DOWN

1 __ dozen (abundant)
2 Say it isn't so
3 Come out
4 Song star Paula
5 Sockless
6 Highland hill
7 Sleepy sign
8 Sound of the West
9 Control-tower staff: Abbr.
10 Scheduling phrase
11 Mockery
12 Airport stats.
15 "You can count __"
18 Seneca's *sum*
20 Chess promotion
24 Leftover
27 "__ way to go!"
28 Flowerless plants
30 Hesitator's syllables
32 Ginnie __
33 Cooking herb
34 Noshed on
35 Barker and Bell
36 Clark Kent or Ratso Rizzo
37 Overwhelm
38 Kind of error
44 "The Duke of Brooklyn"
45 Grown together
46 Tired out
48 Noted Canadian physician
49 Singer Redding
50 Comic actor Aykroyd
52 *Ne plus __*
53 One of those things
55 Genuine
56 __ California
58 Film-set VIP

56 SPECIALIZATIONS

by Randolph Ross

ACROSS

1 Small towns
6 Non-clerical
10 Radar image
14 Biblical patriarch
15 Siam visitor
16 Four-star review
17 Soda-jerk's specialty?
19 Brainstorm
20 Take aback
21 Sought office
22 Marty portrayer
24 Literary initials
26 Cozy
27 Writer's specialty?
33 Path's beginning
34 German article
35 Hang in the balance
37 AP rival
38 Court procedure
41 Golfer's position
42 Full of calories
44 Theater attendee
45 Words to the audience
47 Egyptian's specialty?
50 Lauder rival
51 Female pheasant
52 Fireworks name
55 Be shy
57 Sandy stuff
61 Doozy

62 Tour-guide's specialty?
65 "Pronto!"
66 Sped away
67 Allow to ride
68 Family rooms
69 Chop __
70 Idolize

DOWN

1 Loman's son
2 Voice of America org.
3 Make fun of
4 Newspaper name
5 __-fi
6 Tra trailer
7 Sometime soon
8 "Minuet __"
9 Hot peppers
10 Raise
11 Fill a hold
12 Currier's partner
13 Marsh material
18 Treat with milk
23 Place to be stuck
25 Restaurateur Toots
26 Mexican state
27 Dinner jelly
28 New York city
29 Transcribe again
30 More desperate
31 Archaeological find
32 Bagnold et al.
33 __ Town
36 Actress Wallace Stone

39 Vanity cases
40 Fill
43 Vocal reflexes
46 Got to first base
48 Fox sitcom
49 Guitarist Atkins
52 Bag brand
53 Scheme
54 __ Bator
55 Grimm character
56 Cheese product
58 Mag printing process
59 Fictional aide
60 Tony-winner Daly
63 Chit
64 Slangy suffix

57 TOO WISE FOR YOU

by Shirley Soloway

ACROSS

1 Caesar's sidekick
5 Football play
9 Kind of shark
13 "Famous" cookie maker
14 Picker-upper
15 Moistureless
16 Sour-tasting
17 Wiser, maybe
18 Funny Foxx
19 Dairy-case buy
22 "I've __ up to here!"
23 Bubbled again
27 Anchor's place
30 Slyly disparaging
31 Earring holder
34 Dogpatch patriarch
38 Actor Vigoda
39 Open courtyards
40 Prefix for system
41 Annually
44 Citrus drinks
45 Cosmetics name
46 One with airs
48 Firmly determined
52 Dow Jones component
56 Sunny shade
59 Soft mineral
62 Homeric epic
63 Gymnast Korbut
64 Baseball manager Felipe
65 Clock sounds
66 *Hud* Oscar-winner
67 Become fuzzy
68 Fresh talk
69 Flying piscivore

DOWN

1 Angler's haul
2 Astaire's hometown
3 Prepared apples
4 Straddling
5 Fabric, for short
6 Choice words
7 Prolonged attack
8 Use steel wool
9 Singer Al
10 *People __ Funny*
11 Little goat
12 Out-of-the-ordinary
14 Trifle (with)
20 Hwy.
21 Full of promise
24 Found pleasing
25 Draw out
26 Test recordings
28 Do a vet's job
29 Actress Jurado
31 Paint coat
32 Too heavy
33 Finishes ahead of
35 Judge's intro
36 Zadora et al.
37 Tall story
42 Happen again
43 Eerie Lugosi
44 Colorful shell
47 Miner's find
49 Inventory count
50 Shire of Rocky
51 Ambler and Blore
53 Not as hale
54 Utah city
55 Low-lying land
57 Talks too much
58 PGA distances
59 File-folder feature
60 Winner's take, often
61 Gossett or Gehrig

by Randolph Ross

ACROSS

1 Take notice, maybe
6 Variety-show fare
10 Toy-magnate Schwarz
13 "Take Me __"
14 Braid
15 Matterhorn, e.g.
16 Thinking lucidly
18 Dot on a French map
19 Cools one's heels
20 Slip of a sort
22 Pinpoints
25 Melding game
27 Atlantic islands
28 Get smaller
29 Meted (out)
30 "Entertainment" preceder
31 "When __ door not a door?"
34 Extremities
35 Hot-tempered
36 Oxlike antelopes
37 Society newcomer
38 Rolling, in a way
39 Makes a scene
40 Pop star Richie
42 Et __
43 Wound in a reel
45 Mideast capital
46 Twist of prose
47 Baseball manager Joe
48 It may be spared
49 Kind and generous
55 12/24 or 12/31
56 Clamorous
57 Farm-machine name
58 Actor Beatty
59 Pull (in)
60 Best and Ferber

DOWN

1 Air Force org.
2 Ind. neighbor
3 Lower digit
4 Without warning
5 Like some movies for preteens
6 "Too bad!"
7 No gentleman
8 Overtime reason
9 Patron of Fr.
10 Easily sunburned
11 Parcel out
12 Puccini work
14 Favorites
17 Gets moving
21 Was in charge of
22 Worked on the docks
23 O_3
24 Without remorse
25 Quite careful
26 Bohemian
28 Beach find
30 Installed mosaics
32 *Kama* __
33 Syrian leader
35 Stooge Larry
36 Brought together
38 Crusade, e.g.
39 Mark again
41 Charged atom
42 Relief org.
43 Squad-car feature
44 Make one's case
45 Danish physicist
47 Fed. agent
50 *Bells __ Ringing*
51 *Louis Quatorze* was one
52 First-down yardage
53 Fab competitor
54 __ Moines, IA

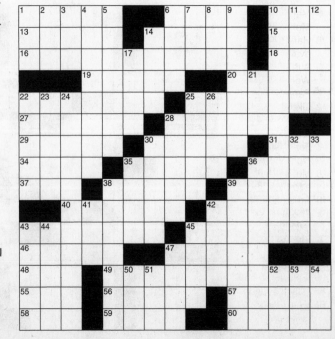

59 KINSHIP

by Cynthia Lyon

ACROSS
1 Art style
5 Put off
10 "What __?"
14 *Lucky Jim* author
15 Toothpicked delicacy
16 Cry of acclaim
17 START OF A QUIP
20 Consoles
21 Coat of arms
22 Joad-family member
23 Went left
26 PART 2 OF QUIP
32 Analyze sentences
33 Skip
34 Spill the beans
36 __-disant
37 Magnani and Moffo
38 Harvarder's rival
39 Austen's Miss Woodhouse
41 Paraphernalia
42 Like __ (50-50)
44 PART 3 OF QUIP
47 Fry's *The __ Not for Burning*
48 Monastery address
49 Arnaz autobio
52 The Syr Darya feeds it
56 END OF QUIP
60 See 8 Down
61 Stable worker
62 Hollywood clashers
63 Baseballer Sandberg
64 Medieval guild
65 Everything else

DOWN
1 Roast table
2 Shot
3 TV knob
4 __ a pig
5 Scale starter
6 Flora in an O'Neill title
7 Little lie
8 One of two raft riders?
9 Pron. type
10 Work on a soundtrack
11 Quitting time for some
12 "A Little Bitty Tear" singer
13 Cutting
18 "__ to bury Caesar . . ."
19 Nation in the Atl.
23 Mass-market books?
24 It's for the birds
25 Long-dist. line
26 *Dixit* lead-in
27 Fashion model Campbell
28 "Donkey Serenade" composer
29 Unfrequented
30 Kate Nelligan film of '85
31 Chic shop
35 Small snack
37 Improved, cheesewise
40 Sinatra tune
42 Kind of comprehension
43 Less
45 Munro's alias
46 "Time will doubt __": Byron
49 Place of worship?
50 Substance
51 Yves St. Laurent's birthplace
52 Bustles
53 Wise one
54 Piccadilly statue
55 A.D.C.
57 I may follow them
58 Refrain fragment
59 Way out there

60 PUN JABS

by Randolph Ross

ACROSS

1 Call for help
4 NFLer, e.g.
7 Angle measure
13 Daley's city, for short
14 Finish third
15 Third of an inning
16 Squealer
17 Indian children's game?
19 Lunchroom lure
21 Tide type
22 Indian stocking stuffer?
26 Long ago
30 Peter, Paul & Mary's "Day __"
31 Bar furnishing
32 Brutus' breakfast?
35 Important time
36 Fraught with pitfalls
37 Indian lunches?
41 Blackmail, perhaps
42 GM auto
43 Compass pt.
44 Bulls and Bears
45 Ocean floor
48 *Garfield* dog
49 Indian pirate flag?
53 Jeff Bridges' brother
55 Habituate
56 Indian farming?
62 Archaeological expedition
63 Toxic substance
64 Gstaad gear
65 "Wow!"
66 Squirrel, for one
67 Beer barrel
68 Pipe shape

DOWN

1 Beanpole
2 Butler's wife
3 Squash, maybe
4 Greek letter
5 Stewart or Serling
6 Use credit
7 Actress Blakley
8 Forever __ day
9 Tyrannical
10 __ *Dalmatians*
11 Razor-billed bird
12 Ultimate degree
14 Persian potentates
18 Green Gables girl
20 16th-century start
23 I.e., for long
24 Mrs. Dithers
25 *I Married __* ('42 film)
27 Nogales night
28 Elton John pitched them
29 *Family Ties* mom
31 Indian honorific
32 "__ Billie Joe"
33 Overwrought
34 Mongolian range
36 __-four (standard plank)
38 Headquarters
39 Taxing org.
40 "Let's shake on it!"
45 Aretha's realm
46 Eastern Indians
47 Cupid or Quayle
49 Pleasure trip
50 Beauty-pageant VIP
51 *The Little Mermaid*
52 German philosopher
54 Wharton subj.
56 Fool's mo.
57 Sticky stuff
58 Be free (of)
59 "For shame!"
60 Mini-guitar
61 Apparatus

61 DON'T WALK

by Fred Piscop

ACROSS

1 Fuel-gauge reading
6 Got blubbery
10 No Honest Abe
14 Comic Anderson
15 Football's __ Alonzo Stagg
16 "*Der __*" (Adenauer)
17 RUN
20 Not fem.
21 *Days of Heaven* star
22 Like week-old bread
23 Moe's cohort
25 Darning __ (dragonfly)
26 War fleets
29 Sow's mate
30 Play reveille
31 Animation frame
32 __ tai cocktail
35 RUN
40 Radical campus org.
41 Att.'s title
42 Consequently
43 Meets with
45 Ceramic servers
47 Decathlon components
50 Craze
51 Joshua of Broadway
52 Sportscaster Albert
53 Ratio phrase
57 RUN
60 "Waiting for the Robert __"
61 Cher ex
62 Quotable catcher
63 X-ray units
64 Goose kin
65 Shady place

DOWN

1 Jr. high preceder
2 "__ Lisa"
3 Propels a shot
4 Haberdashery buy
5 The Beatles' "__ Blues"
6 '40s baseball brothers
7 Rough stuff
8 Lech Walesa, for one
9 Lao-__
10 Second of two
11 Its hero is Achilles
12 Bikini, e.g.
13 Richards of tennis
18 Taj Mahal site
19 Government workers' org.
24 "Zip-__-Doo-Dah"
25 Vincent Lopez's theme
26 Eyebrow shapes
27 Crucifix
28 "__ the word!"
29 Actor Vereen
31 __ au vin
32 __' War (racehorse)
33 C.P.A.
34 Turner and Pappas
36 Golfer's pocketful
37 Feminine suffix
38 Bangkok resident
39 Mr. Fixit
43 Bags
44 Sicilian spewer
45 Game fish
46 #10's, e.g.
47 Bugs' pursuer
48 "Success!"
49 Urged, with "on"
50 Polynesian peak
52 Persian's plaint
54 Belgradian, for one
55 Poi, essentially
56 General Bradley
58 Cable-network letters
59 Unfilled time-slot abbr.

62 FRANKLY SPEAKING

ACROSS

1 Hold up
5 PC owner
9 Flavorful
14 Sonic clone
15 __ contendere
16 Madrid museum
17 START OF A QUIP
20 Doc
21 *Quo Vadis?* role
22 Reuben's bread
23 Mag. execs
24 Wartime offense
26 Actress Freeman
27 It gets letters
32 Finished, in a way
35 Hit the bell
38 *The Neverending Story* author
39 PART 2 OF QUIP
42 Yours, in Tours
43 British servant
44 Continent's dividers
45 Big shot
47 Nix, in a way
49 PART 3 OF QUIP
52 PART 4 OF QUIP
55 Fidel's friend
58 Sgts., e.g.
59 Lower (oneself)
61 END OF QUIP
64 '50s record
65 Insignificant
66 Old one: Ger.
67 Did modeling
68 Some votes
69 Hideout

DOWN

1 "__ Be the One"
2 Felt sore
3 Loses one's coat
4 Writer Morrison
5 Awaiting delivery
6 Acapulco warmer
7 Ms. Verdugo
8 Popular posies
9 Folksy instruments
10 Canine comment
11 *Up to __* ('50s game show)
12 For no reason
13 Senate VIP
18 Army creatures?
19 Animal feeder
25 Planet of the Apes, really
26 College major
28 Film studio, for short
29 "A one __ two . . ."
30 Admired one
31 Chippendale quartet
32 Esau's wife
33 Baum barker
34 One of the Ghostbusters
36 "That's it!"
37 Chutzpah
40 Water partner
41 Square one
46 Gave clues
48 *The Courtship of __ Father*
50 Big-headed, sort of
51 Helena's competitor
52 Inventor Nikola
53 West Indies nation
54 ATM key
55 Pork order
56 Nativity-play prop
57 Remnants
60 Ground grain
62 Stamping machine
63 Top at the pool

63 GROWING THINGS

by Wayne R. Williams

ACROSS

1 Magazine layout
7 Tight spots
11 Have more to say
14 *Ruby* star
15 Brainstorm
16 Martial-arts legend
17 At home
18 Gilding material
20 Shop equipment
21 In a careless way
22 Coffee servers
24 Meat dish
26 Sherlock's hat
30 Unite
33 Woody's son
34 Frog kin
35 __ one's time
36 Division word
37 Does paperwork
38 Israeli guns
39 Free-for-all
40 Ripped up
41 Poker pack
42 Craving
43 Electricity sources
46 William or Sean
47 Singer Wooley
48 Mountain lions
51 Greyhound pacer
55 Skier's maneuver
59 Guarantee
60 Feeling blue
61 Son of Isaac
62 Small sofa
63 Word that filers ignore
64 Landlord's due
65 Word form for "intestine"

DOWN

1 Go to sea
2 __ colada
3 Remainder
4 Peace Nobelist of 1912
5 Birch-family trees
6 Alice __ Live Here Anymore
7 Lively dance
8 Fuss and feathers
9 Gibson or Tillis
10 "The Ballad of the Green Berets" singer
11 Emcee Trebek
12 Business arrangement
13 Challenge
19 Belli's field
23 Took a chair
24 Fleming and Hamill
25 Kennedy and Koppel
26 Holstein's home
27 Bert's buddy
28 John of rock
29 French river
30 Dry up
31 Proclamation
32 Class furniture
35 *Buck Privates* co-star
37 English prep school
43 Annoy
44 *Wheel of Fortune* category
45 Use yeast
46 Actress Dawber
48 Attention-getting sound
49 Home of the Jazz
50 Ancient Persian
52 Scottish island
53 *Champagne* bucket
54 *Vincent & __* ('90 film)
56 Put to work
57 Hightailed it
58 Obsessive fan

64 TASTE TEST

by Scott Marley

ACROSS
1 Kind of chop
5 Trucker, often
9 Guff
13 Western show
14 Bank (on)
15 Aware of
16 Cousteau's domain
17 Make eyes at
18 A Four Corners state
19 Saves
21 Reply to *gràzie*
22 Pub order
23 "__ She Sweet?"
24 Keep score, in cribbage
25 Gielgud's title
26 Watering hole
30 Hobo's dinner
33 Night sight
36 Hunter's need
37 Comic Johnson
38 Kilmer classic
39 Feel no __ (be tipsy)
40 Franklin's flier
41 Quick summary
42 Art Deco name
43 Space-race starter
45 Signs off on
47 Shirt or blouse
48 Be audacious
50 *Playbill* paragraph
53 Like some keys
56 To the __ (all the way)
58 Butter alternative
59 Football score
60 *Arroz* partner

61 Move like a hummingbird
62 __ Eleanor Roosevelt
63 Out-and-out
64 Certain Hindu
65 Honey bunch
66 Annoying one

DOWN
1 Union group
2 Designer Simpson
3 Walnut's innards
4 Dwarf tree
5 Promote, in checkers
6 Bible word
7 Jed Clampett's daughter

8 Ham's mate
9 Poor loser's attitude
10 Put into the pot
11 For men only
12 London district
13 Singer Julius La __
20 Landing place
21 According to
24 Globetrotter's need
25 Fondness for desserts
26 La __ Tar Pits
27 Mr. Sharif
28 Drop off
29 Semiautomatic rifle
30 Fifth Avenue store
31 Fall clumsily

32 Caesarean phrase
34 Difficult journey
35 '60s nuclear agcy.
44 Likewise not
46 Maintain the pace
48 Newsperson Sawyer
49 World book
50 Sings like Merman
51 Small bay
52 Telltale sign
53 Mary Quant and colleagues
54 Jai __
55 Schmo
56 Shade of white
57 Instructional method
59 Yak away

65 PENNY-WISE

by Donna J. Stone

ACROSS

1 Door part
5 Parish priest
10 Roads scholar?
14 Israeli airline
15 __ Gay
16 At any time
17 Moore of *Mortal Thoughts*
18 Get __ (eliminate)
19 Nelson's river
20 START OF A QUIP
23 Soft metal
24 Spruce up
25 Brainy brats?
30 Offer an opinion
34 '75 Wimbledon winner
35 Tipped off
37 *Peanuts* character
38 Menlo Park monogram
39 MIDDLE OF QUIP
41 Tom, for one
42 Striped stone
44 Heavy metal instrument
45 Heart's desire
46 Go over again
48 Acts like Attila
50 Cremona cash, once
52 Actor McShane
53 END OF QUIP
61 Intaglio material
62 Cantaloupe or casaba
63 Easy stride
64 Grimm creature
65 Coeur d'__, ID
66 Brainchild
67 Call the shots

68 Filled to the gills
69 __-do-well

DOWN

1 Champions of the Force
2 Pianist Templeton
3 Early sitcom
4 Crepe cousin
5 Betty's rival
6 "What's __ for me?"
7 Musical postscript
8 Overhead
9 Basket fiber
10 Shakespearean subject
11 *Metamorphoses* author
12 Endless band

13 Hydrox rival
21 Relative of -ist
22 In a weird way
25 Saudi Arabia neighbor
26 Grammarian's concern
27 "Do __ a Waltz?"
28 Take the Pledge?
29 Frame
31 Disguised, for short
32 Smooth-spoken
33 Senator Kefauver
36 Skater Thomas
39 "__ to please"
40 Dumped on
43 Wired, in a way

45 Hand-lotion ingredient
47 Some TV shows
49 On the __ (fleeing)
51 Cub Scout leader
53 Gimlet, but not daiquiri
54 *Picnic* playwright
55 Dame Hess
56 "__ a Song Go . . ."
57 Not a soul
58 Centering point
59 Piece of fencing?
60 Century segment

66 SPICE RACK

by Richard Silvestri

ACROSS

1 Young fellow
4 *War Games* group
9 Scored well on an exam
13 On the rocks
15 Puff up
16 Quite positive
17 Procession VIP
19 Place for corn
20 Examined thoroughly
21 Airline-board info: Abbr.
22 Metal sources
23 16 and 21, e.g.
25 Delight in
27 From the heart
31 Iron man?
34 Cove relative
35 Gentleman's gentleman
37 "What Kind of Fool __?"
38 Comment conclusion
39 British diarist
40 Sinful
41 Ariz. neighbor
42 Dropped pop, e.g.
43 Made away with
44 Threatener's words
46 Rankled
48 Anne, to Margaret
50 German coal region
51 Huck's transport
53 Prefix for skeleton
55 Colored slightly
59 Like crazy
60 Dawdle
62 One of the strings
63 Born first
64 Ear part
65 -kin kin
66 Gary Cooper role
67 A fistful of dollars

DOWN

1 Wilted
2 Rent-__
3 Art follower
4 One in want
5 Ending for scram
6 Hard to get
7 Téte-__
8 Makes mad
9 Cucumber-like?
10 Seek through flattery
11 The __-Lackawanna Railroad
12 American Socialist Eugene
14 Candidate, at times
18 Sired
24 Bank client
26 Trifling amount
27 Manilow's instrument
28 Go in
29 Devil's symbol
30 In the __ luxury
32 M. Zola
33 Got one's goat
36 Guitars' ancestors
39 Came before
40 Timeless
42 Compass pt.
43 Sober-minded
45 Chicken or Rich
47 Bacchus' attendants
49 Nolan's fate
51 Enthusiastic review
52 Got down
54 Antiquated "antiquated"
56 Incandescence
57 Island near Corsica
58 Applied henna
61 Held first

67 THE ELEMENTS

by Wayne R. Williams

ACROSS

1 Canseco or Ferrer
5 Lends a hand
10 NYC cultural attraction
14 Grub
15 Nicholas Gage book
16 From the beginning
17 EARTH
20 Started up: Abbr.
21 Jean Renoir film
22 Tearful woman
26 Emcee's job
30 AIR
34 Board material
35 Classic car
36 Singer Kitt
38 Not fer
39 CIO's partner
40 CCXXV + CCCXXVI
41 Out of sorts
43 Hood's heater
44 Witty remark
46 Dundee of boxing
48 Santa __, CA
49 Up to
51 FIRE
53 Paradisiacal
55 Wish granter
56 French 101 verb
58 "Eye" word form
62 WATER
68 Pitts of comedy
69 Church honoree
70 Highway division
71 Object
72 Turner and Louise
73 Hazzard deputy

DOWN

1 Ballet movement
2 Thole inserts
3 RBI or ERA
4 Juan Carlos' realm
5 *Playboy* nickname
6 "Xanadu" group
7 Superman foe Luthor
8 Nabokov novel
9 Mideast region
10 Hindu sage
11 "Sail __ Ship of State!"
12 Actress Harris
13 Dumbfound
18 Stood for
19 Bancroft or Boleyn
23 Florida city
24 Showing off
25 Erhard's discipline
27 Jamaican music
28 Writer Fallaci
29 Language structure
30 *Violin and Palette* painter
31 Money back
32 Limestone variety
33 Be a bandit
37 William __ White
42 Tanner's need
45 Conifer arbor
47 Band engagement
50 Vilnius' loc.
52 Pester the comic
54 High point
57 Morales of *Bad Boys*
59 __ Bator
60 Late-night name
61 Assayer's material
62 Israeli gun
63 Tended tots
64 Weather-vane dir.
65 Brooch, e.g.
66 Genetic letters
67 Part of TGIF

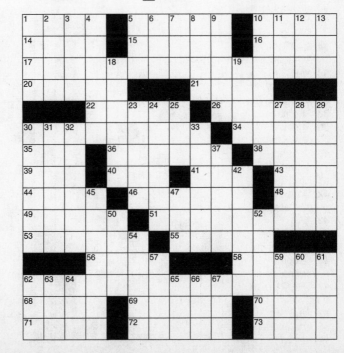

68 MATH ANXIETY

by Randolph Ross

ACROSS

1 Headquarters
6 Most wise
12 Piece of needlework
14 Competed on the Charles
15 Basement entrance
16 Predestines
17 START OF AN OLD JOKE
19 Big Apple initials
20 Dreamer's phenom.
21 Ms. Lupino
24 Arm of the Riviera?
27 Impressionist
29 Signs up
31 __ Palmas
32 Kind of blade
33 Hall-of-Fame pitcher Fingers
34 PART 2 OF JOKE
36 PART 3 OF JOKE
37 Makes up (for)
38 Shortfall
39 Agnew's nickname
40 Contract details
41 Haul away
42 Mamie's predecessor
43 AAA suggestion
44 Taunter's cry
45 Shooter ammo
47 THE PUNCH LINE
53 Pugilist
56 Eye opener?
57 Hôpital resident
58 Soiree time
59 Hollow stones
60 Clear the tape

DOWN

1 Italian port
2 NYSE rival
3 Gives rise to
4 Quarterback John
5 Ocean views
6 Get lost
7 Imported auto
8 Iris' cousin
9 Actor Wallach
10 Sun Yat-__
11 6-pt. plays
12 European airline
13 Scandinavian rug
14 Comparatively steamed
18 Unencumbered
22 Water down
23 Liqueur flavorings
24 Swell up
25 Roof beam
26 Classify
28 Bill-signing souvenir
29 Dallas daddy
30 Tournament placements
32 Arden et al.
33 Open to suggestion
35 Caught in a net
36 Baseball club
38 Bird on a Canadian $1 coin
41 Word of comfort
42 Cereal topper
44 Bakery equipment
46 Fishing specialist
48 Raison d'__
49 Lemony quencher
50 "Oh, what a relief __!"
51 *And Then There Were __*
52 Bit of work
53 Fruit tree
54 Feminine-name ending
55 Onetime sports car

69 HARD TO SWALLOW

by Randolph Ross

ACROSS

1 Knocks for a loop
6 Caesar's 300
9 *King Kong* co-star
13 "It's the end of __!"
14 Parlor, for one
16 Roll-call response
17 Less, in La Paz
18 "__ se habla español"
19 Geometric lines
20 Practiced restraint
23 Lost
27 Shoe holder
30 PC screen
31 Fashionable Drive
32 Tear apart
33 Men and boys
34 Warning signals
35 "Gotcha!"
36 Quilters' convention
37 Middling grade
38 Scale notes
39 Talkative type
41 Talent for music
42 Nastase of tennis
43 Capri and Wight
44 Pod preceder
45 Beatty and Buntline
46 Talked idly
50 Retracted a remark
54 Pasta choice

57 Have __ (know somebody)
58 Actor Patrick
59 Wickedness
60 Stand up to
61 __-car
62 Turns colors
63 Mind-altering drug
64 Wild fancy

DOWN

1 Door frame
2 "Dedicated to the __ Love"
3 Fast time
4 Ran slowly
5 Prokofiev's bird
6 Apple bearer
7 Acts the flirt

8 *The Little Engine That __*
9 A question of motive
10 Reviewer Reed
11 *Diamonds __ Forever*
12 "Without a doubt!"
15 Not at all spicy
21 Artist/illusionist
22 Bizarre
24 Swimmer Gertrude
25 Virgilian epic
26 Plays horseshoes
27 Like *Hamlet*
28 Go over old ground
29 Make possible

34 Letter flourishes
36 Attack on all sides
37 Heel over
40 Moans and groans
41 Immigrants, e.g.
42 Vocalizer
47 Unwilling to listen
48 On key
49 In __ (briefly)
51 Russo of *Lethal Weapon 3*
52 Bank deposit?
53 Verbal attack
54 Londoner's last letter
55 Wall climber
56 Music marking

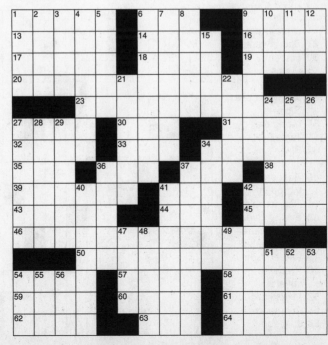

PUNCTUATIVE

by Wayne R. Williams

ACROSS

1 From a distance
5 They're serious
11 Package letters, often
14 Painful
15 Bathroom bottle
16 Word form meaning "sharp"
17 Exodus directive
19 Majors or Marvin
20 Lawrence portrayer
21 Department-store section
23 Major annoyance
24 Aftward
25 Nasal expression
27 Sports venues
30 Forceful trends
33 Prefix for while
35 Jenny in *Love Story*
36 Muckraker Tarbell
37 Sleep inducers
40 Research thoroughly
41 Raised trains
42 Starter chips
43 Gear features
45 Disarm a bull
48 Wheat variety
50 Prepares cutlets
52 Mideast liquor
56 In proportion
58 Just about
59 "Eureka!"
60 Gum-related
63 According to
64 Old Testament prophet
65 Urgent
66 Launch counter?
67 French Revolution leader
68 Gets it

DOWN

1 British racecourse
2 Civil War expert Shelby
3 Knight clothes
4 Deep regret
5 Bucks
6 Measuring stick
7 Nav. rank
8 Bearings
9 Write in the margin
10 Gordon or Irish
11 Portico's companion
12 Cart team
13 Re-colors
18 *The Tempest* king
22 High dudgeon
24 Fills with fizz
26 Hold your horses
28 Came down
29 Sound bored
30 In deadlock
31 Running in neutral
32 Driver's display
34 Pipe part
38 Slender cigar
39 Speaker system
44 Quick trips
46 Bobby of hockey
47 Gathered in
49 Robert of *Soap*
51 "Mack the Knife" singer
53 Bandleader Shaw
54 __ Boothe Luce
55 Rote and Rote, Jr.
56 *Hair* producer
57 Big bird
61 Shakespearean contraction
62 "Now I see!"

71 SILVER LINING

by Donna J. Stone

ACROSS
1 Pugilistic pokes
5 Grating
10 *Casablanca* setting
14 Square measure
15 Bring bliss to
16 Blind as __
17 Analyze poetry
18 Light beer
19 Run the show
20 START OF A QUIP
23 Adams and McClurg
24 Put in stitches
25 __ *Rosenkavalier*
27 Fam. member
28 Hollywood clashers
32 Hardly hyper
34 Proofer's findings
36 In the know
37 MIDDLE OF QUIP
41 Asian desert
42 Legendary quarterback
43 Verdi opera
46 Moon Mullins' brother
47 Antipollution grp.
50 Bear's lair
51 Peter out
53 Diverse
55 END OF QUIP
60 Gooey stuff
61 Join up
62 Part of Batman's garb
63 Coward of drama
64 *Cheers* chair

65 Nautical adverb
66 Creole veggie
67 Celica model
68 Runners carry it

DOWN
1 Artist Johns
2 Give consent
3 __ '66 (Sergio Mendes group)
4 Have a hunch
5 Dean Martin role
6 Jai __
7 Old clothes
8 Sunflower supports
9 Caduceus carrier
10 "__ Mia" ('65 tune)
11 A dime a dozen
12 Tiny Tim's trademark
13 When Strasbourg sizzles
21 Grenoble's river
22 Flock female
26 Auto acronym
29 Terrier threat
30 Iolani Palace locale
31 Reeked
33 Kennel critters
34 Depraved
35 Reebok rival
37 Seven-pound computer
38 Jacob's partner
39 Ending for prior

40 David's great-grandmother
41 Neptune, but not Earth
44 Kapaa keepsake
45 Preoccupy
47 Sing the praises of
48 Mr. Reese
49 Rattled one's cage
52 Namibia native
54 Pizarro victims
56 Oscar __ Renta
57 Play thing
58 Third-rate
59 __ podrida
60 *Starpeace* artist

by Wayne R. Williams

ACROSS

1 Sentence break
5 Change for a five
9 Manhandled
14 Rights grp.
15 Storm the comedienne
16 Actor Milo
17 First Henry Aldrich movie
19 Dueling tools
20 Some anchors and stringers
21 Nonviolent protest
23 Babylonia, today
25 Read a poem
28 Rommel et al.
32 Shoshone tribe
34 Profit figure
35 Boorish one
36 Sore spots
37 Bleacher yell
38 Neck and neck
39 Glynnis O'Connor film
40 Stood up
41 Geom. shape
42 Blue shades
43 Sahara mount
44 Function
45 Roll-call call
46 Isn't colorfast
47 Duke of Edinburgh
49 Ms. Teasdale
51 Like a standoff
53 Priest's hat
58 Stone worker
60 Abbott and Costello film
62 Nonsensical
63 Ireland's alias
64 European capital
65 Rose essence
66 Paramount structures
67 Blossom support

DOWN

1 Tony Orlando's backup
2 Charley horse
3 Shredded side dish
4 Crude dwellings
5 Lustful lookers
6 Mrs. Yeltsin
7 Pixie
8 Gets a load of
9 49 Across, e.g.
10 Spicy jelly
11 Van Johnson movie
12 Wide-shoe letters
13 Pub. defenders' foes
18 __ acids
22 Peaceful Greek
24 Gores' predecessors
26 Back-combed
27 Merman and Barrymore
28 Ocular device
29 Fill with joy
30 David Janssen movie
31 Charged atom
33 Kazurinsky and Conway
36 __ Lap ('83 film)
39 Bawls
40 Actress Charlotte
42 Stephen King novel
43 Mild cigar
46 Half the honeymooners
48 Hotelier Helmsley
50 Scrub a mission
52 She sheep
54 Genesis name
55 Evaluation
56 Roof piece
57 Energy source
58 "Mamma __!"
59 Grasshopper's colleague
61 Hurry up

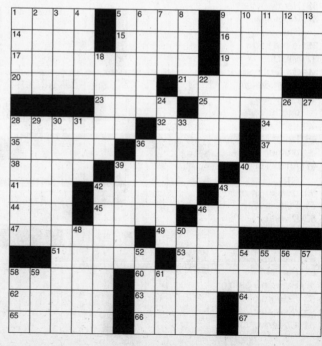

HOW CUTE!

by Trip Payne

ACROSS

1 Color Me __ (pop group)
5 Courtly dance
10 Michigan, e.g.
14 BSA part
15 Ms. Trump
16 Yoked team
17 Lopez's theme
18 Asocial one
19 Parker products
20 SPEAKER OF QUOTE
23 Big ape
24 Houston player
28 Dover dish
31 Half-grown herring
33 Baby food
36 START OF A QUOTE
38 "I smell __!"
40 *Gaslight* star
41 Florida's Miami-__ county
42 MIDDLE OF QUOTE
45 British Airways craft
46 Equestrian's cry
47 Fix typos
49 Prized violin
50 Gets warm
54 END OF QUOTE
60 It brings people closer
63 Compel
64 US alliance
65 See 43 Down
66 Electrolysis particle
67 Statuesque model
68 Marquis or viscount
69 Shows team spirit
70 Ltr. enclosure

DOWN

1 *Deliverance* dueler
2 "My Cherie __"
3 Reese of *The Royal Family*
4 Tuckers out
5 Arizona river
6 What Stratford's on
7 Homestead Act offering
8 Unique item
9 Trim, as expenses
10 Hardly close
11 Firefighter's need
12 Barbie's beau
13 Nav. rank
21 They may be colossal
22 Spineless one
25 Bonet and Simpson
26 Bagnold et al.
27 Convened again
29 Earring spots
30 Ham it up
31 Eydie's singing partner
32 Ran on TV
33 Shells or spirals
34 __ *With a View*
35 Turkish title
37 Pinkerton logo
39 Philanderer
43 With 65 Across, Monty Python member
44 Hirschfeld's daughter
48 Pete Sampras' field
51 *Battlestar Galactica* name
52 Moreno and Coolidge
53 *Basic Instinct* star
55 Worshiping place?
56 Words for Nanette
57 Small band
58 Kilt wearer
59 Sawbucks
60 State follower
61 Wordsworth work
62 Flamenco cry

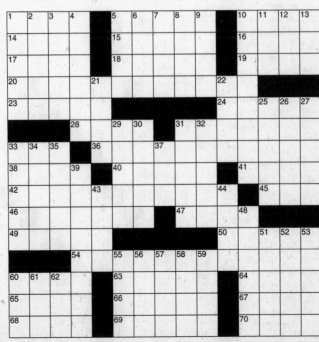

74 WHERE'S MR. LINCOLN?

by Eric Albert

ACROSS

1 Swerve or twist
5 Attorney-___
10 Pillow cover
14 Curb cry
15 Tibetan capital
16 Our Gang dog
17 *Butterfield 8* star
20 Drenched
21 Hardly exciting
22 "Olde" store
23 Highway marker
24 Prepare
25 Virginia, once
28 Babe's bed
29 Holyfield's pride
32 Island greeting
33 Animated character
34 Delany of *China Beach*
35 Filed wrong, maybe
38 Squared away
39 Stand up
40 Director Walsh
41 Above, in verse
42 Cream buy
43 The sky, so to speak
44 Pawn
45 Jupiter's alias
46 Again and yet again
49 FDR's place
50 Shake up
53 Gung-ho expression
56 Finely appointed
57 Packing a rod
58 Barn dance
59 Crude cartel
60 Styne show
61 Brisk

DOWN

1 Lamb dish
2 Green veggie
3 Way to go
4 Expert
5 Hudson River city
6 English homework
7 Past due
8 Timber tree
9 Phone service
10 Secretly observe
11 Samaritan's offering
12 At the zenith
13 Nothing more than
18 Lacking a key
19 Ishmael's boss
23 "Over There" writer
24 Investigate thoroughly
25 Walk-on
26 Green shade
27 Dangerfield persona
28 Run by gravity
29 Informal instrument
30 Better
31 With low spirits
33 Use your noodle
34 Ladd or Lane
36 Bob Barker prop
37 Become broader?
42 Somewhat: Mus.
43 Improv offering
44 Soprano's attainment
45 Is in accord
46 Galley glitch
47 Earring variety
48 Trick
49 Mildly moist
50 Off-road vehicle
51 Declare formally
52 Bank (on)
54 Stab
55 Returns org.

75 INTRODUCTIONS

by Scott Marley

ACROSS

1 Political movement
6 Bar in a car
10 "__ Ha'i"
14 A, as in Athens
15 Like a bishop's move: Abbr.
16 "The doctor __"
17 Classic movie line, supposedly
20 Prefix meaning "outside"
21 Fireplace tool
22 Singer Trini
23 "Get lost!"
24 Qty. of heat
25 Do or sol
27 Have the lead
29 Sound beater?
32 '83 play
36 Soccer target
37 Nightfalls
38 __ upswing (rising)
39 Hit tune of '65
42 *Padre's* sister
43 Contentment
44 Barbershop sound
45 It runs when broken
46 Encouraging remarks
48 Make __ out of (disprove)
51 Earth tremor
53 Armstrong affirmative
56 Cohan tune end
59 To __ (unanimously)
60 *The Wizard* __
61 Gobbled up
62 Outdoor meals, for short
63 Moist, in a way
64 City on the Rhone

DOWN

1 Checked in
2 Actor Karras
3 Till
4 __ Na Na
5 Made of clay
6 *A Bell for* __
7 PED __ (corner sign)
8 Troubadour's repertoire
9 Rational mind
10 Theater name
11 "The earlier, the better!"
12 Occupation
13 Don Juan's mother
18 Gnu home
19 Extreme
23 Copy editor's concern
24 Deep voices
25 Mama Judd
26 Midwest city
27 Set starter
28 Hawaiian idol
29 Mideast region
30 Rascal
31 Lacrosse-team complement
33 "What __!" (bored one's remark)
34 Willie of baseball
35 Beef cuts
36 "Vamoose!"
40 Pola of the silents
41 Pequod survivor
45 Brings home
46 Posh
47 Holmes clue
48 41 Down's captain
49 Helpless one
50 Asian nation
51 Not out
52 Sufficient, in poems
53 Regarding
54 Sign of tomorrow
55 Some dolls
57 George Burns role
58 Scottish river

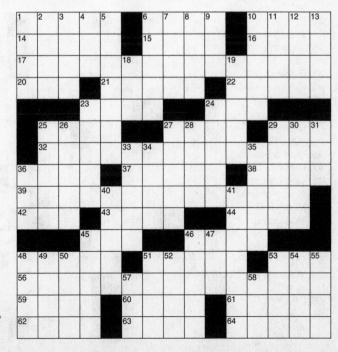

76 POSSESSIONS

by Wayne R. Williams

ACROSS

1 Fiery crime
6 Actor Erwin
9 French priests
14 Martin's toy
16 Ruth's mother-in-law
17 Edith's dessert
18 Diamond boot
19 Ms. Ono
20 Singing voices
22 Fast food
23 Change color
24 Elements
26 Small band
30 Astrologer Sydney
32 Likes a lot
34 Pearl's family
38 Post-WWII strongman
39 *Jagged Edge* star
41 Bigotry
42 C.P.'s gardening tool
44 Drunk as a skunk
46 High times
47 Mimics
48 Magic word
51 *Nova* network
53 Miami team
54 Moe victim
57 To be, to Marie
61 Org.
63 Margaret's joint
65 Office skill
66 Edwin H.'s wrap
67 Ruhr Valley city
68 Half of *deux*
69 Fly-eating bird

DOWN

1 Drained of color
2 Word form for "current"
3 Water well
4 *Novus __ seclorum*
5 PM periods
6 Hackneyed
7 Wrongful act
8 As far as
9 *Wheel of Fortune* buy
10 Red's dance
11 __ acid
12 Chew the scenery
13 Becomes a dad
15 Collar insert
21 Open spots
23 Female rabbit
25 Peeve
26 "Memory" musical
27 Valhalla VIP
28 Lorre role
29 Jerry's pitch
30 Orchestra group
31 Greek M's
33 Training center
35 Welles character
36 Way: Lat.
37 Beatty et al.
40 Either Chaney
43 Tippler
45 Prof.'s aides
48 Look of the moon
49 Takes breaks
50 Does gently
51 Trim a tree
52 West Virginia senator
55 Rights grp.
56 Chestnut horse
57 Ending for opal
58 Spring event
59 Opportune
60 Dueling sword
62 Issue side
64 Recipe meas.

77 ROADSIDE VERSE

by Cathy Millhauser

ACROSS

1 Exile isle
5 Hashhouse spheroid
10 Complaining sort
14 Bartlett or bosc
15 Up __ (stuck)
16 Attract
17 Top of the head
18 Tome home
19 Singer Redding
20 START OF A VERSE
23 5 Across feature
24 Brewer's oven
25 A Bobbsey
26 Retain
27 Dennis' neighbors
31 Make beam
34 Line that isn't there
36 Floral garland
37 PART 2 OF VERSE
41 Director Howard
42 Pot covers
43 Groups of two
44 Necessitates
47 Old oath
48 Genetic material
49 Orion has one
51 Word before sister or story
54 END OF VERSE
59 "__ the mornin'!"
60 Where the blissful walk
61 Livy's love
62 Inventor Sikorsky
63 Handy
64 Slave away
65 A lot
66 Broadway bestowals
67 "Smooth Operator" singer

DOWN

1 __ Lederer (Ann Landers)
2 Spinach descriptor
3 Enjoy the ocean
4 2-D extent
5 South Seas explorer
6 Aramis' colleague
7 Italian city
8 Hard to hold
9 Stain again
10 Troupe group
11 Old Testament name
12 Scotto solo
13 Top-rated
21 Kayak user
22 __ ammoniac (ammonium chloride)
26 Nonprescription: Abbr.
27 Mental faculties
28 Ms. Korbut
29 Requirement
30 Remains idle
31 Rochester's love
32 Doctorow's __ Lake
33 Polly, e.g.
34 Rental name
35 Marked a ballot
38 __ Eve
39 Deles, maybe
40 Comic Louis
45 Shaded spots
46 One-million link
47 Distress signals
49 Conk
50 Post of etiquette
51 Pago Pago's land
52 Egg-shaped
53 Texaco Star Theater star
54 Working hard
55 Order phrase
56 Familiar with
57 Golden Rule word
58 Bartholomew Cubbins' 500

78 A CROSSWORD

by Wayne R. Williams

ACROSS

1 Joke around
5 Fleming and Carney
9 English racecourse
14 Assert positively
15 Stare open-mouthed
16 Take off
17 July 1, in Moose Jaw
19 Tiberius' tongue
20 Not quite right
21 Pencil-box items
23 Take a total
24 Sully
26 Fermi's concern
28 S.A. nation
29 Japanese novelist
33 Trajectories
36 Talked like
38 "Encore presentation"
39 Resting spot
40 *Bolero* composer
42 Scotland __
43 __ *Bulba* (Gogol novel)
45 City on the Arno
46 Deep black
47 George Wallace, for one
49 Cliburn or Morrison
51 Arrived
52 Skycap's tote
56 Actress Arthur
58 Brief bio
61 Coll. basketball tourney
62 Flynn of films
64 Indian chief
66 Board of education?
67 Nordic name
68 Singer Sonny
69 Lab work
70 Gumbo ingredient
71 Album tracks

DOWN

1 Reformer Riis
2 Get around
3 Dispatches
4 La-la lead-in
5 Culture medium
6 Detection device
7 "__ brillig . . ."
8 Actresss Ione
9 Top player
10 __ of Marmara
11 Racing boat
12 *Metamorphoses* author
13 Look after
18 Moose cousin
22 Uncooked
25 Islamic bench
27 Following directions
29 Kline or Costner
30 Fruity quaffs
31 Ottoman
32 *60 Minutes* name
33 Cinema canine
34 Honest-to-goodness
35 Falconlike birds
37 Haydn's nickname
41 South Seas skirt
44 Bakery freebies
48 Debussy's *La __*
50 Teen ending
52 State of India
53 Type of pear
54 James Dean film
55 Cultural spirit
56 Highest-quality
57 Perry's penner
59 Melville novel
60 *Columbo* star
63 Mel of baseball
65 Telephonic 2

79 SING SING

by Trip Payne

ACROSS

1 DeMille production
5 Well-qualified
9 Hoop star Thomas
14 It's undeniable
15 Clothes line?
16 John __ Garner
17 Regrets
18 Barbara Mason tune of '65
20 Actor Wallach
21 "__ Lang Syne"
22 Using chairs
23 Like Poe's stories
25 Small cobras
26 Mr. Wiesel
27 Aid in crime
28 Hitter's stat
31 New World explorer
33 Shutterbug buy
35 Pearl Buck character
36 Sevareid et al.
37 "Dedicated to the __ Love"
38 Beef cut
40 Parachute parts
41 Jimmy's daughter
42 Cool treats
43 Ballet garb
44 Bolger costar
45 Hose material
48 Taxing subject
51 Sisters or mothers
52 Recipe phrase
53 UB40 tune of '88
55 MP's quarry
56 Former Dodge
57 Actress Swenson
58 Back of the neck
59 Library no-no
60 Hideaway
61 Goes blonde

DOWN

1 Zimbalist of *The F.B.I.*
2 Singer Abdul
3 Vanilla Ice tune of '90
4 Dol. parts
5 Guarantee
6 Blues street
7 Alan or Cheryl
8 Dash lengths
9 Kind of interview
10 Long stories
11 "You're soaking __!"
12 Land measure
13 Hung onto
19 Make judgments
21 Slightly
24 Without company
25 How some are taken
27 Wanted-poster word
28 Slade tune of '84
29 Extorted
30 Wading bird
31 Caesar's partner
32 Reunion attendee
33 Less restrained
34 Salvation Army founder
36 Was artistic with acid
39 Popular cat
40 Ornery sort
43 Unmusical quality
44 Bodies of knowledge
45 Molds and mushrooms
46 Take the honey and run
47 *Twice-Told __*
48 OPEC member
49 Rex's sleuth
50 Half of DCCCIV
51 Ricci or Foch
54 Comic Shriner
55 &

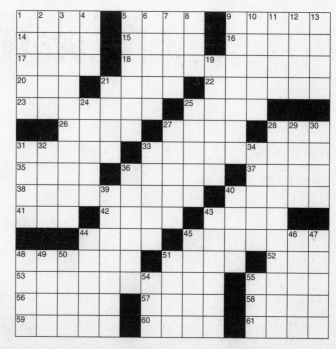

80 STOCK ANSWERS

by Harvey Estes

ACROSS

1 Collins of rock
5 Manner of walking
9 "Excuse me!"
13 Mystical poem
14 Brit's 14 pounds
15 What love may mean
16 Stock company?
18 Miscellany
19 Racy beach?
20 Hollywood hopeful
22 Adored ones
24 Spread in a tub
25 Café cup
28 Soup sample
30 Grump's exclamation
33 *Ordinary People* actor
35 Captures
37 Zsa Zsa's sister
38 Desire deified
39 Apollo 11 module
41 Become boring
42 Damage
43 *M*A*S*H* nurse
44 Sell wholesale
46 Vote in
48 Part of TNT
50 Eat away
51 Porcine meal
53 Entanglement
55 Columbus landfall
58 Hare __
62 U.S.
63 Stock option?
65 Cleo's queendom
66 Musical sounds
67 Peña's passion
68 Well-handled
69 Medium
70 Flintstones' pet

DOWN

1 Stir to action
2 Kona dance
3 Jones' nickname
4 Radicals
5 Makes off with
6 Carload
7 Ultimate aims
8 Spaghetti sauce
9 Portuguese possession
10 Stock exchange?
11 Northeast port
12 Not worth arguing about
14 Word form for "Chinese"
17 Copland ballet score
21 *The Sound of Music* scenery
23 Lounge entertainers
25 Main focus
26 Ear-oriented
27 Stock holder?
29 Chum
31 Flee from
32 Batman's alias
34 S. Dak. neighbor
36 Hyacinth's home
40 SST concern
41 Southern California town
43 Bit of matter
45 Spooky
47 Bordeaux beverage
49 More black
52 Solemn agreements
54 Parentheses' shapes
55 Shortwave, e.g.
56 Gallic girlfriend
57 Smithy's item
59 Sphere starter
60 Inert gas
61 __-*American Symphony* (Still opus)
64 Wee hour

ON FOOT

by Shirley Soloway

ACROSS

1 Skim and 1%
6 Balance center
9 Put together
13 TV studio sign
14 Make eyes at
15 Expended
16 Asian evergreen
18 Barnum's singer
19 Author Bagnold
20 Come after
21 A piece of cake
22 Eastern Indians
24 VT clock setting
26 Gun the engine
27 Infused with zeal
32 Photo
35 Utility device
37 Like lettuce
38 Pueblo material
40 Rap-sheet letters
41 Flynn of films
42 Clunky car
43 Streisand co-star in '91
45 Mao __-tung
46 Hitchcock film of '36
48 Election winners
50 Recipe amt.
51 Lack
55 Pear choice
58 Painter Rembrandt
61 Inflight offering
62 Utah resort
63 British collegians
65 Close loudly
66 Kingly address
67 High-ceiling halls
68 Orchestra member
69 WWII region
70 Finishes ahead of

DOWN

1 Heston role
2 Senseless
3 Bandleader Lester
4 Joking sort
5 Sp. lady
6 Swelled heads
7 Felipe of baseball
8 Cash in
9 Driver of a sort
10 Where most people live
11 Family rooms
12 Sea swirl
14 Keeps
17 GI's time off
23 Bonds together
25 They may be vented
27 Tea type
28 River to the Caspian Sea
29 Move quickly
30 Strange sightings
31 Nabors role
32 Good buddies
33 Inspiration
34 Search thoroughly
36 Sharp flavor
39 Marine base
44 Rome's river
47 Place side by side
49 Mideast resident
51 Spiny houseplant
52 Closes in on
53 "Shut up!"
54 Lanchester and Maxwell
55 Big party
56 __ podrida
57 Lead player
59 Leave the stage
60 Continental prefix
64 Bit of hair cream

82 DIAMOND CRIMES

by Randolph Ross

ACROSS

1 June dance
5 Inferior
9 Allan-__
14 Verdi heroine
15 Skating maneuver
16 Mideast desert
17 What the runner did
20 Picketers, perhaps
21 Wipes out
22 Actor Frobe
23 Applications
24 Vegas hotel
26 Guinness Book suffix
27 Agatha's colleague
31 5th-century pope
32 National spirit
34 Poetic adverb
35 What the third-base coach did
38 Pitch __-hitter
39 Copier chemical
40 Exigencies
41 Laugh heartily
43 Headline of '14
44 Nursery sounds
45 Lends a hand
47 Reagan confidant
48 Harmonize
51 Zeppelin's forte
55 What the slugger did
57 Nosey Parker
58 Fancy wheels
59 S-shaped curve
60 Bullish sound
61 Dance routine
62 Highway

DOWN

1 Written permission
2 Director Martin
3 Skunk's weapon
4 Libeled
5 Sci-fi weapons
6 Put out
7 Short times
8 Thruway warning
9 Conductor Previn
10 Insult
11 Turkish leaders
12 __ majesty (high crime)
13 Nights before
18 Squeezed by
19 Greek sage
23 Wedding-party member
24 Office worker
25 Say OK to
26 The upper atmosphere
28 Richards of tennis
29 It's on the Aire
30 Messes up
31 Persian potentate
32 Lab burners
33 Daily event
36 Snow form
37 One next door
42 Cosmetics queen
44 Drive-in server
46 Unmoving
47 Casino order
48 Bits of current
49 Chance to play
50 The Andrews Sisters, e.g.
51 Mine entrance
52 Shakespearean villain
53 No contest, perhaps
54 Albertville vehicle
56 Chi-town trains

83 FIRST PERSONS

by Wayne R. Williams

ACROSS

1 Union bane
5 Calendar abbr.
9 Tavern orders
14 Unpunctual
15 State with authority
16 Actor Delon
17 Individuals
18 Recent retiree
20 Wedding tradition
22 Harsh-looking
23 In the know
24 Tailor, often
26 Nosed out
28 Roll-call count
30 Speaks grandiloquently
34 Red-headed riot
39 Star's stage
40 Colorado Rockies owner
41 Fellow
42 Chips, at times
43 Seth's son
44 *Kate & Allie* costar
46 Evita's title
49 *Discovery* agcy.
50 Student's souvenirs
53 At the ready
57 Ipanema's locale
60 *North Dallas Forty* star
62 Author Benchley
63 Reagan aide
66 Folk tales
67 Nicholas Gage book
68 Govt. training pgm.
69 Margot role
70 Thickheaded
71 Waste allowance
72 Poetic works

DOWN

1 Indolence
2 Tippy transport
3 Mr. T and crew
4 Miss America of '45
5 Actor Mineo
6 Arden et al.
7 Pro golfer Calvin
8 Group of three
9 One with the funds
10 "Xanadu" rockers
11 For one
12 Edgar __ Burroughs
13 Crackle's colleague
19 Mythical ship
21 Rains cats and dogs
25 Actress Charlotte
27 *The Purple Rose of Cairo* actor
29 Epic tale
31 Lug around
32 At any time
33 Fresh language
34 Hotshot pilots
35 Nary a one
36 Palindromic time
37 Capek play
38 Hebrew letter
42 Famed fabler
45 Atlas page
47 What Nancy called her hubby
48 Ion source
51 Choose
52 Handle the helm
54 Got up
55 Spooky
56 Prepare for work
57 Musical mouthpiece
58 Not busy
59 Author Wister
61 Spanish direction
64 Officeholders
65 Dig in

84 FARM TEAM

by Wayne R. Williams

ACROSS

1 Take up
6 Antonym: Abbr.
9 Jack the dieter
14 Jason's wife
15 Aussie leaper
16 Dress style
17 British actress Joan
19 Makes a scene
20 Sun. speech
21 Inventor Nikola
22 Pampas backdrop
23 Train unit
24 Diplomacy
26 Really enjoy
29 Like some farm animals
34 Currency-exchange fee
35 Arafat's grp.
36 Switch on
37 Abrasive tool
38 Not as polite
40 To be, in Toulouse
41 One-celled animal
43 Tax agcy.
44 Poverty
45 Very scary
47 Tries out
48 Sothern and Sheridan
49 Track action
50 Let up
53 Little green man
56 Actress MacGraw
59 Sound
60 Hull collection
62 *The Maltese Falcon* actress
63 Greek letter
64 *Cannery Row* star
65 Rock-strewn
66 Cariou of musicals
67 Poke fun at

DOWN

1 Rock-concert gear
2 Remove from text
3 Fragrance
4 Basilica bench
5 Kind of sauce
6 Assns.
7 Sci-fi writer Frederik
8 It may be hot
9 Crusader's opponent
10 British royal house
11 Outer covering
12 Pot starter
13 Hardy heroine
18 Cash ending
23 Joint effort
25 Mimics
26 Fergie's first name
27 Old World lizard
28 Cap part
29 TV actor Gulager
30 *The Age of Bronze* sculptor
31 Merits
32 Long-plumed bird
33 Property records
35 Shrimp kin
39 Unit of work
42 Parched
46 Señora Perón
47 One renting
49 Pa Cartwright
50 Gardner et al.
51 Rope fiber
52 Singing voice
54 Past due
55 Pro boxer Barkley
56 __ breve
57 "Why not?"
58 Comment of clarity
61 Iowa college

85 ENGLISH MAJORS

by Randolph Ross

ACROSS

1 They're often exchanged
5 __ Raton, FL
9 Asian priest
13 Gulf state
14 Gem weight
15 Riviera seasons
16 Stead
17 Clear as __
18 They fly by night
19 Raven rhymester?
22 Big belly
23 Concert closers
24 Letter getter
29 Negotiations
30 Rhyming wisecracker?
32 Ring result
33 Menlo Park monogram
34 Ms. MacGraw
37 Actress doing screenplays?
43 Minneapolis suburb
45 New hires
46 Salon work
48 Peak
49 Autobiographer president?
54 Disassemble
55 Leans (toward)
56 Given the boot
58 Slay
59 George of *Star Trek*
60 Ship out
61 Nine-digit IDs
62 H H H
63 Extremities

DOWN

1 Actor Kilmer
2 Garfield's canine pal
3 Unwelcome growth
4 Cozy up
5 Rum cake
6 Pitcher Hershiser
7 Spanish street
8 Home of the Hawks
9 Maestro Stokowski
10 Busy
11 Free-for-alls
12 ADCs
14 Egg holder
20 Subtle glow
21 Sen. Helms' state
24 *A-Team* actor
25 NASA assent
26 Bar's beginning
27 In the know about
28 Had in mind
31 Yogi, for one
34 Went to Wendy's
35 *To Kill a Mockingbird* author
36 Auditing org.
37 Dennis' neighbors
38 Monogram part: Abbr.
39 Ms. Fabray
40 '60s dance
41 Something hysterical
42 Synchronous
43 Cultural group
44 __-the-wool
46 Desert Storm targets
47 Tony the Tiger's favorite word
50 "Times of your Life" singer
51 Citrus drinks
52 Draft team
53 Tear apart
57 Tooth pro's deg.

86 ON CUE

by Matt Gaffney

ACROSS

1 Shriver of tennis
4 "Delicious!"
7 Obi-Wan, for one
11 De Niro role
13 Smooth
15 50-year-old
17 Hypnotized
18 Smoke, for short
19 JFK's predecessor
20 Shake, in prescriptions
21 Strength
24 __ majesty (sovereign crime)
25 Wine word
26 Debater of '92
27 Yearned (for)
28 Run-of-the-mill
29 Pizarro victim
30 Southwest city
33 Nutrition stats.
34 Santa __
35 Heartless one
36 Glide on ice
37 B&O stop
40 High point
41 Moriarty's creator
42 K-6
43 Promulgate
44 *Flying Down to* __
45 In unison
46 Onetime NHL team
51 Touch-and-go
52 Leads
53 Sundance's love
54 LAX client
55 Questioning comments

DOWN

1 Dive in
2 Low-pH
3 *Olympia* painter
4 Pronoun with two homonyms
5 Actress Merkel
6 Ryan or Foster
7 Discombobulate
8 Prints, perhaps
9 World's lowest lake
10 Destitute
11 Blue shades
12 O followers
13 Nasty mood
14 Witchlike woman
16 Real, in Regensburg
21 Course listing
22 Basra's land
23 Happy-__
24 *Peanuts* character
26 Budweiser rival
27 Arouse ire
28 Nonchalant
30 TV's Batman
31 Mideast carrier
32 Unit charge
33 Loser's demand
35 Pyrenees resident
36 Any minute now
37 Pushover
38 Group principles
39 In __ (disheveled)
41 Chop up
42 -ish relative
44 Grid official
45 Lend a hand
47 Lea plea
48 UN Day mo.
49 Ducat word
50 Genetic material

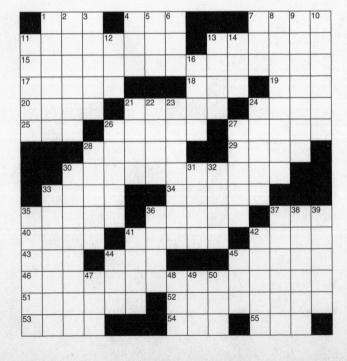

87 FAMILY TV

by Mark Ryder

ACROSS

1 Extensive
5 Saharan transport
10 PBS science show
14 Come up against
15 "What __ is this": Pepys
16 Actor Bates
17 Classic '50s sitcom
20 Go for it
21 Revealing pictures
22 Score part
23 GI address
24 Yale student
25 '60s Arden sitcom
34 Distorts
35 Sale condition
36 Storm or Gordon
37 The Big Band __
38 Snitch
41 Parts of qts.
42 Exxon's former name
44 __ gin fizz
45 Perturb
47 '70s Natwick detective drama
50 Shipping unit
51 Govt. purchasing org.
52 Closet hangings
54 Singer Cleo
57 P.O. poster people
60 TV psychologist
63 Polynesian carving
64 Kid-lit elephant
65 Mr. Roberts
66 Realtor's sign
67 Chevy __, MD
68 In the past

DOWN

1 Travel, as an aroma
2 Construction piece
3 It may call
4 Ordinal ending
5 Metaphorical temptation
6 "Diana" singer
7 More than a few
8 Personalities' parts
9 Actor Ayres
10 Arrester's activity
11 Tub in the fridge
12 Flower holder
13 Industrious insect
18 __ facto (retroactively)
19 One-person performances
23 Fuse unit
24 To be: Lat.
25 Sing like the birdies sing
26 Irritating
27 Clear a tape
28 *Little Iodine* cartoonist Jimmy
29 Bar legally
30 Irks
31 Boo-boo
32 Take in, e.g.
33 Adam and Rebecca
39 ". . . unto us __ is given"
40 Autumn apple
43 Bonelike
46 School org.
48 A bit too interested
49 Pay no mind to
52 Work for three
53 H-M link
54 Jacob's first wife
55 Eban of Israel
56 Tax-deferred accts.
57 Flowerless plant
58 Bric-a-__
59 Global speck
60 Wino's bane
61 Ont. network
62 "Yoo-__!"

88 PLACE NAMES

by Wayne R. Williams

ACROSS

1 Hostess Perle
6 Homecoming attendees
11 Tie-up
14 Blood of the gods
15 Thurmond and Archibald
16 Shoshonean
17 Actress from Peking?
19 Mauna __
20 Sound a horn
21 Troop's camp
22 Window ledge
23 Tiny amounts
25 Sand bars
27 Kind of assault
30 After-shower powder
31 Hasty flight
32 Word form for "skull"
35 Western lake
38 Composer Khachaturian
40 Iberian river
42 Ship of 1492
43 Columbus' home
45 Uses a fork
47 French article
48 Be up and about
50 Proximate
52 On land
54 Warren Beatty role
55 Lead player
56 Rocky debris
58 False god
62 Comparative ending
63 Film director from Warsaw?
65 "Agnus __"
66 Zoo beast
67 Missouri mountains
68 Sprightly character
69 Stair post
70 *Corrida* beasts

DOWN

1 GM's home
2 Reverberation
3 Kicker's target
4 Asia's Gulf of __
5 Coach Parseghian
6 Playwright from Vientiane?
7 Vesuvian flows
8 Texas sch.
9 Slightest
10 123-45-6789 org.
11 Cook from Santiago?
12 Coral ring
13 What American Plan includes
18 Slow down
22 Large seabird
24 Where some stks. trade
26 Bowler or boater
27 Get tired
28 Few and far between
29 Actor from Muscat?
33 Weirdo
34 Tennis pro from Teheran?
36 Till contents
37 Bridge position
39 It's under the hood
41 Toed the line
44 Make public
46 Blue
49 Do cobbling
51 Nixon pal
52 Stage whisper
53 Girder material
54 Construction machine
57 Hammer part
59 From a distance
60 Bushy do
61 Albanian currency
63 Pig's digs
64 Tiny amount

ACROSS

1 *Blondie* boy
5 100 centavos
9 Just for this
14 Slay
15 Declare true
16 *Thelma & Louise* name
17 Lollygag
19 Put up with
20 START OF A QUIP
22 Gathers up grain
23 Be obliged
24 Part of TGIF
27 Carrie Nation, e.g.
28 Overly sentimental
31 Had in mind?
32 Seed or germ
34 Sulu, on *Star Trek*
35 MIDDLE OF QUIP
40 Column order
41 Kind of daisy
42 S&L concern
43 Actress Moorehead
45 Popinjay
48 __-jongg
49 Seaport, for short
50 Troop group
52 END OF QUIP
57 Riyadh resident
59 Judo award
60 *Glengarry Glen Ross* star
61 "Rama __ Ding Dong"
62 Sacred cow
63 Religious devotion
64 Recedes
65 London gallery

DOWN

1 Composer Elgar
2 Do-nothing
3 Lose for a bit
4 Available
5 Forest way
6 Not at all noble
7 18-wheeler
8 Nevada neighbor
9 Playing marble
10 Salami seller
11 Cold capital
12 Sean Lennon's mom
13 Crow cry
18 Start's start
21 Rte.
25 Marky Mark fan
26 Big gulp
28 Speak lovingly
29 Bobby of hockey
30 Party's purpose, perhaps
31 Comedian Stubby
32 Huff
33 Cpl.'s inferior
34 Make an attempt
35 __ Bede
36 Caesar's partner
37 Ferdinand was one
38 Cancel suddenly
39 Dos' followers
43 Succor
44 Talk turkey?
45 Peanuts character
46 Wild cat
47 Club-shaped tool
49 Pluvial
50 Boggy ground
51 Moon's track
53 Mark copy
54 Fine steed
55 Pyramid, essentially
56 Christmas-poem beginning
57 Somebody's fool
58 Onassis, informally

90 VIRTUOUS PEOPLE

by Randolph Ross

ACROSS

1 Sea "king"
5 Goya subject
9 Invites to the penthouse
14 Apollo's mother
15 Get an __ effort
16 Glorify
17 Obsessed by
18 "__ first you don't . . ."
19 Imported auto
20 Virtuous newswoman?
23 Iraqi money
24 "__ live and breathe!"
25 __-cat (winter vehicle)
26 Stanford-Binet scores
29 Point of view
31 Campus mil. grp.
33 Tropical isle
34 Ordinal ending
36 Cardboard creations
38 Virtuous film buddies?
41 Witty exchange
42 Big bird
43 Russian city
44 Sea dogs
46 Carrying a carbine
50 Buddhist sect
51 Military address
52 Have the title
54 Santa __, CA
55 Virtuous Neil Simon character?
58 *Amerika* writer
61 La Scala solo
62 Touched down
63 Back way
64 Apply wax to
65 Countdown end
66 Comic-book cries
67 Cast opening?
68 Idyllic place

DOWN

1 Dover attraction
2 Fix a carpenter's mistake
3 Legendary conqueror
4 Italy's shape
5 Milkers of song
6 *An __ to Remember*
7 Shaw title character
8 Creative
9 Opening word
10 Wood choppers
11 Jazz instrument
12 Eskimo knife
13 Gal. parts
21 Mad milliner
22 Concert bonus
26 Piece of poetry
27 Wharf
28 Bro's sib
30 High country
32 More peculiar
33 Conductor Kurt
35 *Panama __* (Merman musical)
37 __ clef (fiction genre)
38 Roll response
39 Ready for retailing
40 Asian region
41 Russell's nickname
45 Church party
47 Posted
48 All-inclusive
49 Wright brothers' hometown
51 Changes another's mind
53 Marine mammal
55 Turn aside
56 Shoe holder
57 Knock down
58 Arthurian knight
59 Hearty brew
60 Mr. Ziegfeld

91 BEAUTIFICATION

by Alex Vaughn

ACROSS

1 Sweet side dishes
5 West Point mascot
9 Marsh wader
14 "There oughta be __!"
15 Large land mass
16 Make ecstatic
17 Holding forth on the good old days
20 Hamlet's title
21 Be lacking
22 Try to learn
23 Driving game
25 Blithe romp
27 Faux __
30 Trudge through mud
32 Most achy
36 Hockey great's nickname
38 Taj Mahal site
40 Pound portion
41 Paragons
44 Alaskan art form
45 Pup's protest
46 Breathe quickly
47 Russian plain
49 Scissorhands portrayer
51 Noun suffix
52 Star in Cetus
54 Vaccine pioneer
56 Peak A/C time
59 Dried up
61 Televised ribbings
65 Shea Stadium's locale
68 First name in photography
69 Designer von Furstenberg
70 Jai __
71 Disheveled
72 Didn't hang onto
73 Did hang onto

DOWN

1 Uncouth cry
2 Controversial orchard spray
3 Ankle-length
4 Big Band music
5 Strait man
6 Nimitz's org.
7 Largest shareholder?
8 Three-legged stand
9 Clearance height
10 Building wing
11 Shankar specialty
12 Birdsong of basketball
13 Bottle part
18 Sgts. and cpls.
19 Afternoon events
24 Socked in
26 Big Bertha's maker
27 Those who bug
28 Like __ (fast)
29 Nastiness
31 Midas' quality
33 China's Chou __
34 Part of the Lauder line
35 Short-tempered
37 Early aft.
39 Car bars
42 With a saucy twinkle
43 Plain to see
48 "... __ saw Elba"
50 Clear of snow
53 Synthetic fiber
55 Ketchikan craft
56 A remote distance
57 Arm bone
58 Puff of wind
60 Frozen-waffle name
62 Cod alternative
63 Loaded question
64 Playlet
66 In readiness
67 Discouraging words

ACROSS

1 More, to Morales
4 Resort activity
8 SMU's home
14 Worshiper of a sort
16 Set properly
17 Sorrowful, in music
18 Gas figure
19 Canine comments
20 Medieval singer
22 Snick-and-__ (old knife)
23 Suffix for pun
25 *In* __ (actually: Lat.)
26 Meal prayer
28 Lasting impression
31 Soggy ground
33 National League park
35 Howard of *GWTW*
39 Wallach or Whitney
40 Tonal qualities
42 Indy Jones' quest
43 Worships
45 Tax-free bond, briefly
46 *Norma* __
47 Ms. Bombeck
49 Lean one
51 Spoiled kid
54 Ore. neighbor
56 Advanced degs.
59 Recurring verses
62 Vault

63 Eurasian language group
64 Tiny Tim's range
68 Tailor's tool
69 Ran
70 Play up
71 Change the decor
72 Wordsworth work

DOWN

1 Exemplar of greed
2 Embellish
3 Vocal exercise
4 Needle-nosed fish
5 Word form for "ear"
6 Guitarist Paul
7 Wharton hero
8 Scot's preposition
9 Eyebrow shapes
10 Pup groups
11 Women's mag
12 Frank and Tyler
13 Inscribed stone
15 The hare, for one
21 4/15 payee
23 Disunion
24 Pour profusely
27 Fall flower
29 Grip tightly
30 Norse pantheon
31 Actress Arthur
32 "__ Hickory" (Jackson)
34 Defensive weapon: Abbr.

36 Slow tempo
37 Novelist Levin
38 __ out a living
41 Actor Tamblyn
44 Make a second swap
48 Grain beard
50 Cop __
51 Grain coverings
52 Find a new tenant
53 Following
55 With regard to
57 Passé
58 China name
60 Feels poorly
61 Sews up
65 Tailless mammal
66 Ran first
67 Sellout sign

93 SEASONING

by Matt Gaffney

ACROSS

1 LP speed
4 Botch the job
10 Angkor __
13 __ *Girls* (2004 movie)
15 Diner, e.g.
16 Vow words
17 Rock's "Boss"
19 Certain sister
20 National Leaguer
21 In a nifty way
23 Will ritual
28 Suggestion start
29 Moral obligation
32 Salami shop
33 Card game
34 I, as in Innsbruck
35 __ the finish
36 Puttin'-Ritz link
39 Flamenco shout
40 Return
42 A question of method
43 Decathlete Johnson
45 Dealing with a full deck
46 Application
47 Ramsgate refreshment
48 Author Ludwig
49 Mars' alias
50 Woes
52 Passed a law
54 *Le Roi* __ (Louis XIV)
56 Most important
59 Silly Putty holder
60 Queen of disco

66 __ de toilette
67 Sedative
68 Except for
69 One or more
70 Horseshoes shot
71 To catch a thief

DOWN

1 *6 __ Riv Vu*
2 Cartoon skunk Le Pew
3 Engels' colleague
4 Command to Spot
5 __ Cruces, NM
6 Mel of baseball
7 Miniscule
8 Peace goddess
9 Actress Daly
10 Swiss city
11 Grown-up
12 Neil Simon collection
14 Rather cold
18 Swed. neighbor
22 Rachins of *L.A. Law*
24 Garfield's pal
25 Clinton Cabinet member
26 First state, alphabetically
27 Immense
29 Fashion name
30 *Daily Bruin* publisher
31 Lee Majors series
33 Chinese cooker
37 Footwear
38 Wool-coat owners
40 Coll. srs.' test
41 Boston NBAer
44 Alternatively
49 Revolutionary Sam
50 Prediction start
51 Boston's airport
52 Run off, in a way
53 Grounded Aussie
55 Admired one
57 "__ Old Cowhand"
58 Leningrad's river
61 Singer Peeples
62 A Bobbsey
63 Wolfed down
64 Rev.'s address
65 Civil War soldier

94 TREE TOWNS

by Randolph Ross

ACROSS

1 Winds do it
5 Lose buoyancy
9 Fixes the outcome
13 Skywalker's mentor
14 Mötley __ (rock group)
15 Author Ferber
16 Physical, for one
17 Actress Veronica
19 Business arrangement
20 City near Little Rock
23 Imported auto
25 Hawks' org.
26 Where Sonny Bono was mayor
31 Iron in the rough
32 Trig ratios
33 Author Bombeck
36 Craggy ridges
38 Sault __ Marie, MI
39 "Phooey!"
40 Perturbed mood
41 Dandelions, e.g.
43 CPR expert
44 2nd largest Hawkeye city
48 Poetic night
49 Postman's path
50 Atomic research center
56 Square measure
57 Actress Braga
58 Stephen King beast
62 Engird
63 Difficult situation
64 Easily bruised items
65 Fill fully
66 Midmonth day
67 Mother and daughter

DOWN

1 Parting word
2 Smoked salmon
3 Harem quarters
4 Bead money
5 Slivovitz or aquavit
6 Dies __
7 Desensitize
8 Capsize, with "over"
9 Obviously embarrassed
10 Light bulb, symbolically
11 Snarl
12 Breakthrough bacteriologist
18 Inhalers of a sort
21 Treas. Dept. agcy.
22 Football positions: Abbr.
23 Carradine, in *The Ten Commandments*
24 Man of the cloth
26 Garden-store supply
27 Stage platform
28 Prefix for cede
29 "I __ drink!"
30 Run in
34 Ike's missus
35 "__ boy!"
37 Ship accomodations
41 Magic sticks
42 Big ranches
45 "Agnus __"
46 Charged atom
47 Coneheads?
50 Shell propellers
51 Scotto solo
52 Reeve role
53 Asian desert
54 Author Bagnold
55 Pitchfork part
59 "That's yucky!"
60 Coffee, so to speak
61 CIA precursor

95 SAY WHAT?

by Shirley Soloway

ACROSS

1 Part of ABM
5 Hoss' big brother
9 Union bane
13 Sea of Tranquillity site
14 Dressed to the __
16 El __, TX
17 Good goose?
19 Chimp snack
20 Greet, in a way
21 Adaptable
23 Inform performers?
26 Type widths
27 Drill sergeant's syllable
30 Vaudevillian Tanguay
31 First shepherd
33 Actor Roberts
35 Falls from grace
37 ... __ Man, Charlie Brown
40 Wide neckwear
42 Baton Rouge sch.
43 Start of 37 Across
44 Harness horse
45 Feinstein and Clinton: Abbr.
47 Reach across
48 Hebrew month
50 Piece of the action
51 TV's Tarzan
52 Part of PST
54 Veggie buy?
58 Cookery genre
60 Free
64 Bank (on)
65 Doctor duo?
68 Running in neutral
69 Carved stone
70 Considerably
71 Spring times
72 Tributes in verse
73 Sawbucks

DOWN

1 Rock-concert gear
2 Author Ephron
3 Plane, but not train
4 Contribution of ideas
5 Half of LA
6 Prefix for meter
7 Former governor Richards
8 Jason's wife
9 Hot tubs
10 Are forbidden to run off?
11 Gomez Addams portrayer
12 Some pears
15 Nacho topping
18 Eroded
22 No longer a threat
24 Lesser of two __
25 Jose of baseball
27 Bucket of bolts
28 Bear: Lat.
29 Get lucky in one's choice?
32 Self-images
34 Like some dorms
36 First light
38 Kind of exam
39 Say it's false
41 Make an outline
46 Marks of infamy
49 Rubs roughly
52 Curtain fabric
53 Bara of silents
55 "Super!"
56 Two-way preposition
57 Peace Prize sharer
59 Louis and Carrie
61 Floor covering
62 Sacred image
63 Sleek fliers
66 Radical
67 Tabard Inn serving

96 FULL DECK

by Matt Gaffney

ACROSS

1 Basic skills
5 Sea World attraction
10 Lounge around
14 Boxing match
15 Fireballer Ryan
16 Muscat's locale
17 Stadium feature
20 Crooner Garfunkel
21 Stretches the truth
22 Flower holders
23 Like Nash's lama
25 Mass response
27 *White Palace* star
31 Legal matter
34 *St. __ Fire*
35 "The King"
36 Actor Wallach
37 Pie __ mode
38 Senator Specter
39 Medication instrn.
40 Actor Beatty
41 Glue guy
42 Astronomer Tycho
44 CBS symbol
45 "Yeah, tell me about it!"
47 Borscht ingredient
48 Jai __
49 Committee type
52 Bluish-white element
54 "Eureka!"
57 #1 hit by 35 Across
61 Choir voice
62 Spree
63 Tide type
64 "*Très __*!"
65 Animal's track
66 Christiania, today

DOWN

1 "Dancing Queen" group
2 Wild hog
3 Specially-designed
4 Sault __ Marie, MI
5 Escargots
6 Duffer's target
7 Start of a Shakespeare title
8 Satire magazine
9 Cycle starter
10 *Death of a Salesman* character
11 Andy's pal
12 Author Grey
13 Wraps up
18 React to a sneeze
19 Declares positively
24 Recent, in combinations
25 Comment upon
26 Chow __
27 Stateswoman Kirkpatrick
28 Kirstie of *Cheers*
29 Give the go-ahead
30 *Manhattan* director
31 Gets back
32 Nobelist Root
33 Half a cassette
38 Soothing plant
41 Escape button
42 Spew smoke, as a volcano
43 GE acquisition
46 Long for
47 Element #5
49 *Moby-Dick* captain
50 Sandwich shop
51 Can't stand
52 Founder of Stoicism
53 *Othello* villain
55 Get better
56 Purina rival
58 Gun pellets
59 Move like lightning
60 Lennon's lady

97 NET ANATOMY

by Wayne R. Williams

ACROSS

1 Drops dramatically
6 Eyed lasciviously
11 Lumberjack's tool
14 Stand by
15 Wharton character
16 Coach Parseghian
17 Where the strings are
19 Study
20 *Our Man in Havana* author
21 Capriati's weapon
23 Track figures
24 CO clock setting
26 Garbo and Scacchi
27 Appropriate
28 Game units
29 Lobber's target
34 Follow closely
38 Kukla's friend
39 Evergreen tree
40 Break in the audience
41 St. Paul, once
42 Service error
44 Fail to hit
47 Do-it-yourself purchase
48 Least
51 Cave-dwelling fish
52 View quickly
56 Smashing shot
58 Theatrical group
60 Court divider
61 Hacker's malady
63 Sked abbr.
64 Church feature
65 Ward off
66 Farm enclosure
67 Actress Della
68 Nuisances

DOWN

1 Singer Donna
2 Oscar, e.g.
3 Spiked the punch
4 Is partial to
5 Anna of *Nana*
6 Slightly askew
7 Political payoff
8 Wacky
9 Come forth
10 Namib or Negev
11 Former Egyptian leader
12 Sports venue
13 Magic sticks
18 Musical pace
22 Greek hearth goddess
25 Packs to capacity
27 Perfect service
28 Seles swing
29 Jackson and Derek
30 So. state
31 Actor Gulager
32 "Trees" poet
33 *Blame It on __*
35 Sun Devils sch.
36 Out of sorts
37 Voided serve
40 Sternward
43 Pinball miscues
45 Beatty/Hoffman movie
46 Founder of *The Tatler*
48 Lisa and others?
49 Navratilova rival
50 Make a second attempt
51 Ferber and Best
52 Figure out
53 Sugar shapes
54 Nautical direction
55 Small salamanders
57 Poker stake
59 Swing a sickle
62 Wrath

98 BORED GAME

by Donna J. Stone

ACROSS

1 Prudhomme's cuisine
6 Took off
10 Pianist Templeton
14 Bryant or Ekberg
15 Valhalla villain
16 Lower California
17 Valhalla VIP
18 Perfect place
19 Does Little work
20 START OF A QUIP
23 Dug in
25 "For shame!"
26 Like a lummox
27 Rake over the coals
29 English diarist
31 Mosey along
32 Manuscript book
33 Service member?
36 Act like Etna
37 MIDDLE OF QUIP
38 Physicist Niels
39 Take everything
40 __ apso
41 Stimulate
42 New Hampshire campus
43 Job security
44 Right-fielder Tony
46 Halloween decoration
47 Actor Carmichael
48 END OF QUIP
52 Toto's creator
53 Gray or Moran
54 "The Man Without a Country"
57 Grimm creature
58 Bring down the house
59 Grenoble's river
60 Sidereal, e.g.
61 Petty clash?
62 Selling point

DOWN

1 Cornfield cry
2 Pitch __-hitter
3 '40s dance
4 Hatch's home
5 Actress Fabray
6 Sweeney Todd's street
7 City near Stockton
8 Gets by, with "out"
9 Manitoba's capital
10 Puts down
11 Accept eagerly
12 Tape-deck button
13 "The Man in Black"
21 Wish undone
22 Jet-black
23 Discombobulate
24 Conductor's concern
28 Fish-and-chips quaff
29 Self-confidence
30 Author Ferber
32 *The Black Camel* sleuth
33 __ St. Jacques
34 *Star Trek* character
35 Gussy up
37 Play grounds?
38 Coal container
40 Stubbs or Strauss
41 Porky's pal
42 Val of *Thunderheart*
43 Smidgen
44 Inedible orange
45 Singer Branigan
46 "John Brown's Body" poet
48 "__ Named Sue"
49 Rope in
50 Ms. Minnelli
51 It's often total
55 *Hearts __ Wild*
56 Gladiator's item

99 VOWEL CLUB

by Shirley Soloway

ACROSS

1 Wilander of tennis
5 Horse's gait
9 Bank grants
14 Touched down
15 Director Clair
16 Nepal's neighbor
17 Individual performance
18 Heron kin
19 Blows a horn
20 PAT
23 Driver's purchase
24 Easy desserts?
25 *Tonight Show* host
27 Marching musicians
30 Soaks up
33 Cell part
34 Word form for "Chinese"
36 Feathered missile
37 Bovine bellow
38 PUT
41 Actor's signal
42 Remnants
44 Uris or Trotsky
45 Take the podium
47 Guinness statistics
49 Calorie counter
50 Tony relative
51 Letter enc.
52 In the past
54 PIT
60 Theodore of *The Defiant Ones*
62 Night light?

63 "I Want __ Happy"
64 Coeur d'__, ID
65 Sleuth Wolfe
66 Actor Richard
67 Uncovered
68 "So be it!"
69 South African currency

DOWN

1 Opposite of fem.
2 Baseball Manager Felipe
3 Lean to one side
4 Bent over
5 Family groups
6 Picture puzzle
7 Step __ (hurry)

8 Try out
9 Petrol measures
10 Mrs. Lennon
11 PET
12 Naldi of the silents
13 Answer back
21 Lets go
22 Funny bone's locale
26 Doze off
27 Hall of __ (sports star)
28 Hole __ (ace)
29 POT
30 Ever's partner
31 He's no gentleman
32 Take the reins
34 Canonized *Mlles.*

35 Wedding words
39 Church official
40 Rock music, to some
43 Show sorrow
46 Come back in
48 Plundered
49 Man-made fabric
51 Gaze steadily
52 Rhyme scheme
53 Southwestern lizard
55 Annapolis inst.
56 Single unit
57 Caesar's garb
58 Abba of Israel
59 Tear apart
61 Chemical ending

BODY LANGUAGE

by Donna J. Stone

ACROSS

1 North Eur. airline
4 Military materials
9 Bosc alternative
14 "Evil Woman" rockers
15 Hazardous gas
16 Circus jugglers
17 *Diamond* __
18 Puppetry?
20 Novelist Binchy
22 Tallow source
23 Descend upon
26 Import tax
30 Oust from office
32 Tire type
34 Drink like a dachshund
36 Calcutta clothes
38 Busybody
39 Montreal player
41 Michelangelo masterpiece
43 Ice-cream ingredient
44 As a companion
46 Tremble
48 Caribou kin
49 Batman and Rin Tin Tin
51 Undercoat
53 Meryl of *Death Becomes Her*
55 Football equipment
58 Spineless
60 Get to
61 Lips?
67 Skater Midori
68 Muscat native
69 Peachy-keen
70 *Wayne's World* word
71 Frawley role
72 Actress Burstyn
73 Sect starter

DOWN

1 Alabama city
2 *America's Most Wanted* info
3 Shoe?
4 Cubbins' creator
5 College bowl roar
6 Big scene
7 Gift wrap items
8 Newfoundland's
9 Auto accessory
10 PBS benefactor
11 Actress Smithers
12 Time-honored
13 Nav. designation
19 Cold feet
21 Allied vehicle
24 Hippety-hop
25 Aziz of Iraq
27 Brainchild
28 Nail polish?
29 __ *Attraction*
31 Traffic jam
33 High old time
34 Rachel's sister
35 Wheel shafts
37 Very simple
40 __ about
42 Related
45 "Holy cow!"
47 "The Sage of Concord"
50 Trickle
52 Shoe width
54 Pamphleteer Thomas
56 Part owner?
57 Gandhi garb
59 Boat bottom
61 She's tops with Pops
62 Doolittle's digs
63 Former Mideast alliance: Abbr.
64 Big bang letters
65 Presidential nickname
66 Sedan season

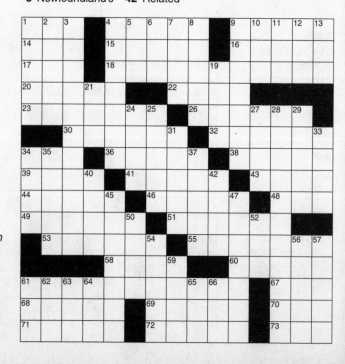

ANSWERS

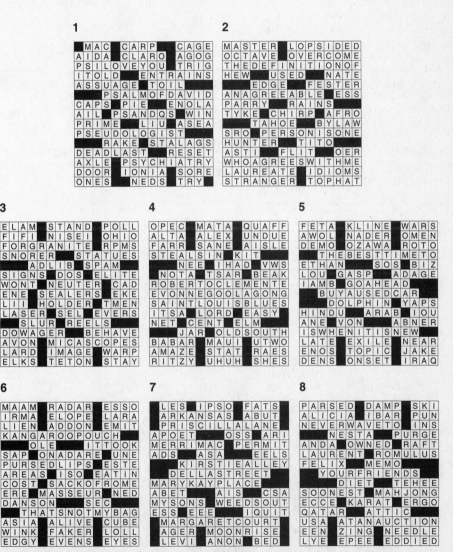

1

M A C	C A R P		C A G E
A I D A	C L A R O		A G O G
P S I L O V E Y O U		T R I G
I T O L D		E N T R A I N S
A S S U A G E		T O I L
	P S A L M O F D A V I D
C A P S	P I E	E N O L A
A I L	P S A N D Q S	W I N
P R I M E	L I U	A S E A
P S E U D O L O G I S T
	R A K E	S T A L A G S
D E A D L A S T		R E S E T
A X L E	P S Y C H I A T R Y
D O O R	I O N I A	S O R E
O N E S		N E D S	T R Y

2

| M A S T E R | L O P S I D E D |
| O C T A V E | O V E R C O M E |
| T H E D E F I N I T I O N O F |
H E W	U S E D	N A T E
	E D G E	F E S T E R
A N A G R E E A B L E	E S S
P A R R Y	R A I N S
T Y K E	C H I R P	A F R O
T A H O E	B Y L A W
S R O	P E R S O N I S O N E
H U N T E R	T I T O
A S T I	F L I T	O E R
W H O A G R E E S W I T H M E
L A U R E A T E	I D I O M S
S T R A N G E R	T O P H A T

3

E L A M	S T A N D	P O L L
F I F I	N I S E I	O H I O
F O R G R A N I T E	R P M S
S N O R E R	S T A T U E S
	A D L I B	S P A M
S I G N S	D O S	E L I T E
W O N T	N E U T E R	C A D
E N E	S E A L E R S	E K E
L I I	H O L D E R	T M E N
L A S E R	S E L	E V E R S
	S L U R	R E E L S
D O W A G E R	B E H A V E
A V O N	M I C A S C O P E S
L A R D	I M A G E	W A R P
E L K S	T E T O N	S T A Y

4

O P E C	M A T A	Q U A F F
A L T A	A L E X	U N D U E
F A R R	S A N E	A I S L E
S T E A L S I N	K I T
N E E	I H A D	V W S
N O T A	T S A R	B E A K
R O B E R T O C L E M E N T E
E V O N N E G O O L A G O N G
S A I N T L O U I S B L U E S
I T S A	L O R D	E A S Y
N E T	C E N T	E L M
J A R	O L D S O U T H
B A B A R	M A U I	U T W O
A M A Z E	S T A T	R A E S
R I T Z Y	U H U H	S H E S

5

F E T A	K L I N E	W A R S
A W O L	N A D E R	O M E N
D E M O	O Z A W A	R O T O
T H E B E S T T I M E T O
E T H A N	S O S	B I Z
L O U	G A S P	A D A G E
I A M B	G O A H E A D
B U Y A U S E D C A R
D O L P H I N	Y A P S
H I N D U	A R A B	I O U
A N E	V O N	A B N E R
I S W H E N I T I S N E W
L A T E	E X I L E	N E A R
E N O S	T O P I C	J A K E
D E N S	O N S E T	I R A Q

6

M A A M	R A D A R	E S S O
I R M A	E L O P E	L A R A
L I E N	A D D O N	E M I T
K A N G A R O O P O U C H
O L E	I T T O O K
S A P	O N A D A R E	U N E
P U R S E D L I P S	E S T E
A R E A S	I S O	E A T I N
C O S T	S A C K O F R O M E
E R E	M A S S E U R	N E D
D A N S O N	S E C
T H A T S N O T M Y B A G
A S I A	A L I V E	C U B E
W I N K	F A K E R	L O L L
E D G Y	E V E N S	E Y E S

7

| L E S | I P S O | F A T S |
| A R K A N S A S | A B U T |
| P R I S C I L L A L A N E |
A P O E T	O S S	A R I
M E R R I M A C	P E R M I T
A D S	A S A	E E L S
K I R S T I E A L L E Y
D E L L A S T R E E T
M A R Y K A Y P L A C E
A B E T	A I S	C S A
M Y S O N S	W E E D S O U T
E S S	E E E	I Q U I T
M A R G A R E T C O U R T
A G E R	M O O N R I S E
L E V I	A N O N	B E D

8

P A R S E D	D A M P	S K I
A L I C I A	I B A R	P U N
N E V E R W A V E T O	I N S
N E S T A	P U R G E
A N D A	O W N E D	R A F T
L A U R E N T	R O M U L U S
F E L I X	M E M O
Y O U R F R I E N D S
D I E T	T E H E E
S O O N E S T	M A H J O N G
E C C E	K A R A T	E R G O
Q A T A R	A T T I C
U S A	A T A N A U C T I O N
E E N	Z I N G	N E E D L E
L Y E	E P E E	E D D I E D

9

S	A	M		B	I	B			D	A	M	A	S	K
P	L	A	Y	E	D	A	T		A	P	A	C	H	E
A	D	M	O	N	I	S	H		P	I	T	M	E	N
R	E	B	U	T		S	E	C		A	T	E	S	T
S	N	O	B		N	E	U	R	O	N	E			
			E	A	R	T	H	E	N		R	A	S	P
M	A	N	T	R	A		E	S		O	N	T	O	
O	B	E	Y	S		C	U	P		A	F	T	E	R
	D	E	V	O		O	O	H		N	I	C	E	N	E
E	S	A	U		S	A	G	U	A	R	O			
			R	E	S	T	I	N	G		U	S	P	S
C	O	A	L	S		I	R	S		C	R	E	A	K
O	N	S	I	T	E		L	A	M	A	S	E	R	Y
L	E	A	F	E	D		S	I	X	P	E	N	C	E
T	A	P	E	R	S			D	I	E		O	H	S

10

A	L	F	A			S	W	E	E	P		R	A	W
D	I	A	N	A		T	I	A	R	A		A	L	A
A	S	S	I	S	T	A	N	T	E	D	I	T	O	R
M	P	H		W	E	N	D			S	T	U	N	
		I	M	A	N		O	R	D	E	A	L		
A	M	O	U	N	T		W	A	I	L		E	S	P
R	A	N	D		D	Y	E	S		S	T	E		
M	I	D	D	L	E	W	E	S	T	E	R	N	E	R
O	N	E		E	R	I	C		Y	A	N	K		
R	E	S		N	I	N	O		S	H	A	K	O	S
		I	R	O	N	E	R		R	O	S	E		
U	R	G	E		A	U	T	O		B	A	T		
S	A	N	D	B	E	L	T	M	A	C	H	I	N	E
E	V	E		S	L	O	O	P		H	A	T	E	D
S	I	R		C	O	O	R	S		Y	E	W	S	

11

P	R	A	M		D	E	C	A	L		T	O	L	L
D	O	D	O		E	X	U	D	E		I	G	E	T
Q	U	A	D		L	I	S	Z	T		M	R	E	D
	E	Y	E	O	F	T	H	E	T	I	B	E	R	
			N	U	T				S	T	U			
P	E	C	A	N		A	H	A		A	K	R	O	N
E	R	A		C	A	S	A	B	A		T	E	N	A
S	O	M	M	E	T	H	I	N	S	T	U	P	I	D
O	D	E	R		T	E	R	E	S	A		A	C	E
S	E	A	L	S		S	Y	R		B	O	Y	E	R
			O	A	F				W	O	O			
	Y	A	N	G	T	Z	E	D	O	O	D	L	E	
J	O	V	E		D	A	V	I	D		L	A	Z	Y
I	D	O	L		I	N	A	N	E		E	T	R	E
M	A	N	Y		X	E	N	O	N		S	E	A	T

12

	E	S	C	A	P	E		A	B	A	L	O	N	E
O	T	T	O	M	A	N		R	A	R	I	T	A	N
C	H	A	S	I	N	G	R	A	I	N	B	O	W	S
H	A	R	T	S			E	L	L	I	E			
O	N	T		H	A	F	T		S	E	L	E	C	T
	E	S	P		W	O	R	M			R	O	E	
			L	I	L	L	I	E		A	T	I	M	E
I	M	P	O	S	S	I	B	L	E	D	R	E	A	M
N	E	A	T	H		O	U	T	L	A	Y			
C	D	I		S	T	E	M		A	R	S			
H	E	R	M	A	N		I	D	O	S		E	M	O
	A	R	E	T	O		A	S	P	I	C			
F	O	U	N	T	A	I	N	O	F	Y	O	U	T	H
A	R	M	O	I	R	E		D	E	N	O	T	E	S
R	E	P	R	E	S	S		E	M	O	T	E	S	

13

J	E	T		H	E	D	Y		M	C	H	A	L	E
O	R	A	T	O	R	I	O		E	N	A	M	E	L
S	I	D	E	W	A	L	K		N	O	R	M	A	L
H	E	A	R	T	S	L	O	C	A	T	I	O	N	
			R	O	E		E	T	E					
E	S	P	Y		A	V	O	W		P	R	A	M	
M	I	A		O	S	L	O		O	T	O	O	L	E
C	O	N	T	E	M	P	T	B	R	E	E	D	E	R
E	U	D	O	R	A		E	L	K	E		E	R	G
E	X	A	M		R	E	S	T		D	O	T	E	
			S	T	S		E	W	E					
M	I	L	E	E	Q	U	I	V	A	L	E	N	T	
R	E	G	A	I	N		C	R	E	D	I	T	O	R
L	A	O	T	Z	U		L	O	N	E	S	O	M	E
S	T	R	E	E	P		A	N	T	S		N	E	E

14

A	D	J		Z	E	T	A		A	L	E	N	E	
L	E	A		E	D	A	M		B	U	X	O	M	
I	F	Y	O	U	D	O	A	J	O	B	T	O	O	
A	B	A	C	U	S			T	A	V	E	R	N	
F	A	C	E	T		A	T	O	N	E		A	D	E
A	B	E	E		E	X	I	L	E		S	C	A	R
R	A	D		T	E	E	N		S	A	T	Y	R	
			W	E	L	L	Y	O	U	L	L			
A	M	A	H	L		T	A	R	O		Q	U	A	
M	A	N	Y		Z	A	I	R	E		B	U	N	S
P	E	N		P	A	L	M	S		M	O	I	R	A
W	A	T	U	S	I		C	A	T	N	A	P		
G	E	T	S	T	U	C	K	W	I	T	H	I	T	
A	S	T	A	B		E	A	R	N		E	N	E	
S	T	O	R	Y		S	T	Y	E		R	E	D	

15

	F	A	R		P	I	T	S		S	E	L	M	A
P	I	T	Y		I	S	E	E		O	N	I	O	N
O	G	R	E		S	L	A	T		A	R	D	E	N
P	H	I	B	E	T	A	K	A	P	P	A			
S	T	A	R	D	O	M		E	S	P	R	I	T	
			E	I	N		R	N	S		T	O	R	O
S	H	O	A	T		M	I	A	O	W		A	A	A
M	I	N	D	O	N	E	S	P	S	A	N	D	Q	S
E	N	E		R	O	S	E	S		P	O	S	I	T
A	G	A	L		N	A	N		S	I	N			
R	E	L	A	T	E		P	A	T	S	I	E	S	
			D	I	T	D	I	T	D	I	T	D	A	H
A	B	O	D	E		A	G	E	D		I	A	M	A
S	A	L	E	M		M	O	R	E		C	H	E	W
P	A	D	R	E		E	T	O	N		K	O	S	

16

H	A	M	S		F	R	E	D		A	L	D	E	R
A	B	A	T		O	I	L	Y		R	E	E	V	E
R	O	N	A		C	O	I	N		G	A	T	E	D
P	U	L	L	W	I	T	H	A	R	O	P	E		
S	T	Y	L	I		S	U	M	O		N	R	A	
			S	T	S			I	N	C	I	T	E	R
A	S	I		A	B	E	T		I	L	I	U	M	
R	O	M	A	N	N	U	M	E	R	A	L	O	N	E
C	A	M	R	Y		T	O	D	O		N	E	D	
E	V	I	D	E	N	T		Y	A	W				
D	E	G		B	E	A	U		N	A	T	T	Y	
	R	E	G	A	R	D	S	A	S	T	R	U	E	
S	H	A	V	E		F	A	U	X		T	A	L	L
O	U	T	I	E		A	L	A	E		L	I	S	P
W	H	E	L	K		T	E	L	L		E	T	A	S

17

	S	P	I	R	E		R	A	D	I	A	L	S	
C	A	R	N	A	L		A	N	A	T	H	E	M	A
P	R	I	N	T	S	O	F	T	H	I	E	V	E	S
R	I	S	E		A	S	T	O		S	M	E	L	T
	S	E	E		P	E	N	T			E	L	I	
M	A	I	D	M	A	R	R	Y	I	N	G			
A	T	E		I	D	E	S		M	O	O	R	E	S
M	I	S	A	L	L	Y		N	I	R	V	A	N	A
A	C	T	I	I	I	I		D	O	N	T		Z	I	P
			R	O	B	B	I	N	G	H	O	O	D	S
U	H	F		S	A	V	E		S	U	R			
S	O	R	T	S		R	I	O	S		T	B	A	R
S	H	E	R	W	O	O	D	F	L	O	R	I	S	T
R	O	S	E	A	N	N	E		U	V	U	L	A	E
S	H	Y	N	E	S	S		M	A	N	L	Y		

18

A	S	K	S		O	F	F	S		A	L	P	O	
S	P	O	T		S	P	A	R	E		J	O	A	N
P	A	C	E		H	E	L	E	N		A	N	T	E
	T	H	E	W	O	R	L	D	S	E	R	I	E	S
			L	A	P		D	E	L					
A	N	E		S	T	O	G	Y		E	L	A	T	E
L	O	L	A		O	R	O		S	N	O	R	E	D
T	R	I	C	K	O	R	T	R	E	A	T	I	N	G
A	M	O	R	A	L		T	O	A		S	A	S	E
R	A	T	E	R		M	A	N	N	A		S	E	R
			E	A	U		P	A	T					
R	A	K	I	N	G	U	P	L	E	A	V	E	S	
A	M	I	N		A	M	O	O	N		S	T	A	T
V	E	N	D		R	U	N	I	N		E	T	C	H
I	N	K	Y		N	U	Y	S		T	A	K	E	

19

A	S	H	E		E	P	A		S	A	F	E	S	T
S	H	O	R	T	C	U	T		P	R	A	Y	E	D
C	U	T	S	H	O	R	T		R	I	S	E	R	S
O	T	T	E	R		I	N	M	O	S	T			
T	U	E		O	P	T		O	U	T	B	A	C	K
S	P	A		N	A	Y		S	T	A	R	M	A	N
			B	E	T		A	E	S		E	A	S	E
W	E	A	R	S		A	S	S		D	A	N	T	E
E	L	L	E		C	O	P		O	A	K			
E	L	E	A	N	O	R		C	A	Y		O	R	B
B	A	C	K	O	U	T		O	R	C		C	O	O
			F	O	R	A	G	E		A	S	T	O	R
T	R	I	A	D	S		O	V	E	R	T	A	K	E
H	A	S	S	L	E		T	A	K	E	O	V	E	R
E	M	O	T	E	S		O	L	E		W	E	D	S

20

B	L	O	T		F	E	A	R		S	P	E	E	D
Y	A	M	S		B	A	J	A		H	O	R	D	E
S	L	E	E	P	I	S	A	N		A	L	I	E	N
E	A	G	L	E		E	X	C	E	L	L	E	N	T
A	W	A	I	T	S		H	A	L	T				
			O	S	C	A	R		T	W	A	N	G	Y
J	E	S	T		O	H	O	H		E	X	I	L	E
A	L	I		W	A	Y	O	F		C	U	L		
P	A	N	D	A		B	A	W	L		B	E	E	P
E	N	G	U	L	F		L	L	A	M	A			
			S	L	A	M		K	I	S	S	M	E	
L	I	S	T	E	N	I	N	G		R	E	T	A	G
A	R	O	M	A		T	O	A	N	O	P	E	R	A
G	O	F	O	R		T	O	M	E		A	V	I	D
S	N	A	P	S		S	K	E	W		Y	E	A	S

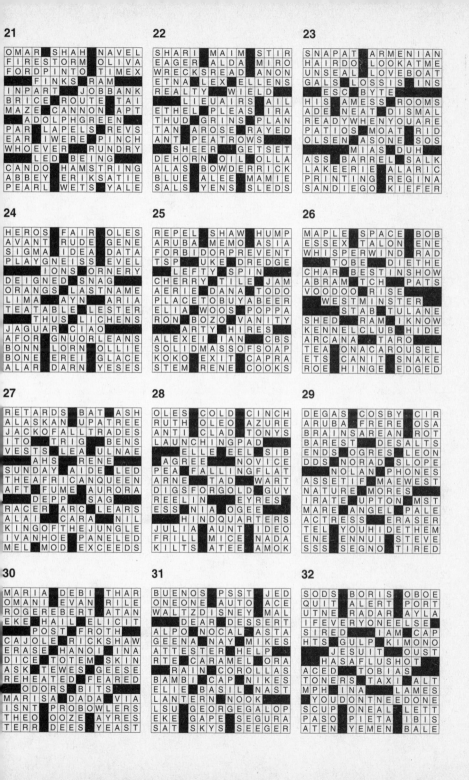

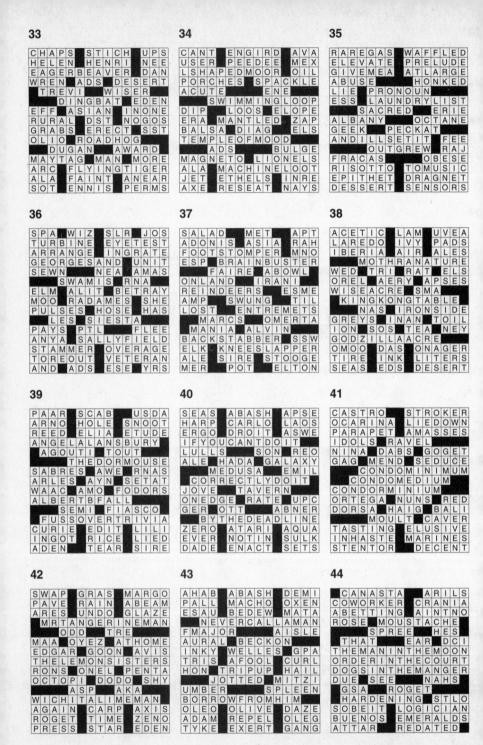

33

CHAPS·STICH·UPS / HELEN·HENRI·NEE / EAGERBEAVER·DAN / WREN·ADS·DESERT / ··TREVI··WISER·· / ·DINGBAT··EDEN· / EFF·ASIAN·INONE / RURAL·DST·NOGOS / GRABS·ERECT·SST / ·OLIO·ROADHOG·· / ··DUGAN··AWARD· / MAYTAG·MAN·MORE / ARC·FLYINGTIGER / ALA·FAINT·ANEAR / SOT·ENNIS·PERMS

34

CANT·ENGIRD·AVA / USER·PEEDEE·MEX / LSHAPEDMOOR·OIL / PORCHES·SPACKLE / ACUTE·····ENE·· / ··SWIMMINGLOOP· / DIP··LOOS·ELOPE / ERA·MANTLED·ZAP / BALSA·DIAG··ELS / TEMPLEOFMOOD·· / ·ADS·····BULGE· / MAGNETO·LIONELS / ALA·MACHINELOOT / JET·ETHELS·INRE / AXE·RESEAT·NAYS

35

RAREGAS·WAFFLED / ELEVATE·PRELUDE / GIVEMEA·ATLARGE / ABUSE···HONKED· / LIE·PRONOUN···· / ESS·LAUNDRYLIST / ···SACRED··ERIE / ·ALBANY·OCTANE· / GEEK··PECKAT··· / ANDILLSETIT·FEE / ····OUTGREW·RAJ / ·FRACAS···OBESE / RISOTTO·TOMUSIC / EPITHET·DRAGNET / DESSERT·SENSORS

36

SPA·WIZ·SLR·JOS / TURBINE·EYETEST / ARRANGE·INGRATE / GEORGESAND·UNIT / SEWN··NEA··AMAS / ··SWAMIS··RNA·· / ELM·ALIT·BETRAY / MOO·RADAMES·SHE / PULSES·HOSE·HAS / ··LES··SIESTA·· / PAYS··PTL··FLEE / ANYA·SALLYFIELD / STAMMER·OVERAGE / TOREOUT·VETERAN / AND·ADS·ESE·YRS

37

SALAD··MET··APT / ADONIS·ASIA·RAH / FOOTSTOMPER·MNO / ESP·BRAINBUSTER / ···FAIRE·ABOWL· / ONLAND···IRANI· / REINDEERS··ESME / AMP··SWUNG···TIL / LOST·ENTREMETS· / ·MARCS··OMERTA· / ·MANIA··ALVIN·· / BACKSTABBER·SSW / ELK·KNEESLAPPER / ALE··SIRE·STOOGE / MER··POT··ELTON

38

ACETIC·LAM·UVEA / LAREDO·IVY·PADS / IBERIA·AIR·ALES / ··MOTHRANATURE· / WED·TRI·RAT·ELS / OREL·AERY·APSES / WISEACRE··SMA·· / ·KINGKONGTABLE· / ··NAS··IRONSIDE / GREYS·INAN·TOIL / ION·SOS·TEA·NEY / ·GODZILLAACRE·· / OMOO·DAS·ONAGER / TIRE·INK·LITERS / SEAS·EDS·DESERT

39

PAAR··SCAB··USDA / ARNO·HOLE·SNOOT / REED·ELIA·ETUDE / ANGELALANSBURY· / ·AGOUTI··TOUT·· / ···THEDORMOUSE· / SABRES·AWE·RNAS / ARLES·AYN·SETAT / WAAC·AMO·FODORS / ·ALBERTBFALL··· / ·SEMI···FIASCO· / FUSSOVERTRIVIA· / CURIE·EDIT·LILI / INGOT·RICE·LIED / ADEN··TEAR·SIRE

40

SEAS·ABASH·APSE / HARP·CARLO·LAOS / ERGO·DROIT·ASWE / IFYOUCANTDOIT· / LULLS·SON··REO· / ALE·HADA·GALAXY / ··MEDUSA··EMIL· / ·CORRECTLYDOIT· / ·JOVE··TAVERN·· / ONEDGE·RATE·UPC / GER·OTT··ABNER· / ·BYTHEDEADLINE / ZERO·ATARI·AQUA / EVER·NOTIN·SULK / DADE·ENACT·SETS

41

CASTRO··STROKER / OCARINA·LIEDOWN / PARAPET·AMASSES / IDOLS···RAVEL·· / NINA·DABS·GOGET / GAG·MEND·SEDUCE / ·CONDOMINIMUM· / ·CONDOMEDIUM·· / CONDORMINIUM· / ORTEGA·NUNS·RED / DORSA·HAIG·BALI / ··MOULT··CAVER· / TASTING·ELUSIVE / INHASTE·MARINES / STENTOR·DECENT

42

SWAP·GRAS·MARGO / PAVE·RAIN·ABEAM / ARES·UNDO·GLAZE / ·MRTANGERINEMAN / ··ODD····TRE··· / MAA·OYEZ·ATHOME / EDGAR·GOON·AVIS / THELEMONSISTERS / RONS·ONEL·PENTA / OCTOPI·DODO·SHY / ···ASP···AKA··· / WICHITALIMEMAN· / AGAIN·CARP·AXIS / ROGET·TIME·ZENO / PRESS·STAR·EDEN

43

AHAB·ABASH·DEMI / PALL·MACHO·OXEN / ESAU·BEDEW·MATA / ·NEVERCALLAMAN· / FMAJOR···AISLE / AURAL··BECKON·· / INKY·WELLES·GPA / TRIS·AFOOL·CURL / HON·TRIPUP·HAIL / ··JOTTED··MITZI / UMBER···SPLEEN· / ·BORROWFROMHIM· / OLEO·OLIVE·DAZE / ADAM·REPEL·OLEG / TYKE·EXERT·GANG

44

·CANASTA··ARILS / COWORKER·CRANIA / ABETTING·AINTNO / ROSE··MOUSTACHE / ···SPREE···HES· / THAT··EAR··DCI· / THEMANINTHEMOON / ORDERINTHECOURT / DOGSINTHEMANGER / ·DUE··SEE··NAHS / ·GSA···ROGET··· / HARDENING··STLO / SOBEIT·LOGICIAN / BUENOS·EMERALDS / ATTAR··REDATED·

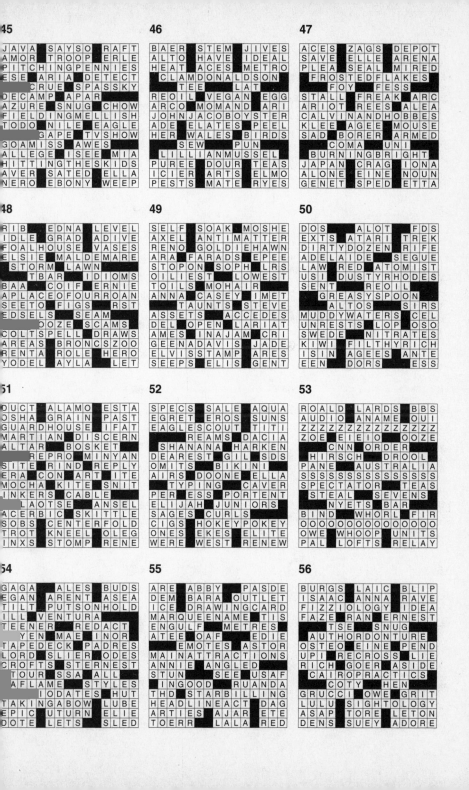

45

```
JAVA  SAYSO  RAFT
AMOR  TROOP  ERLE
PITCHINGPENNIES
ESE  ARIA  DETECT
   CRUE  SPASSKY
DECAMP  APAR
AZURE  SNUG  CHOW
FIELDINGMELLISH
TODO  NILE  EAGLE
GAPE  TVSHOW
GOAMISS  AWES
ALLEGE  ISEE  MIA
HITTINGTHESKIDS
AVER  SATED  ELLA
NERO  EBONY  WEEP
```

46

```
BAER  STEM  JIVES
ALTO  HAVE  IDEAL
HEAT  ACES  METRO
 CLAMDONALDSON
    TEE   LAT
REOIL  VEGAN  EGG
ARCO  MOMAND  ARI
JOHNJACOBOYSTER
ADE  ELATES  PEEL
HER  WALES  BIRDS
   SEW   PUN
 LILLIANMUSSEL
PUREE  DOUR  TEAS
ICIER  ARTS  ELMO
PESTS  MATE  RYES
```

47

```
ACES  ZAGS  DEPOT
SAVE  ELLE  ARENA
PLEA  SEAL  MIRED
 FROSTEDFLAKES
   FOY   FESS
STALL  FREAK  ARC
ARIOT  REES  ALEA
CALVINANDHOBBES
KLEE  AGEE  MOUSE
SAD  BORER  ARMED
   COMA   UNI
 BURNINGBRIGHT
JAPAN  CRAG  IONA
ALONE  EINE  NOUN
GENET  SPED  ETTA
```

48

```
RIB  EDNA  LEVEL
IDLE  GRAD  ADIVE
FOALHOUSE  VASES
ELSIE  MALDEMARE
 STORM  LAWN
  TBAR  IDIOMS
BAA  COIF  ERNIE
APLACEOFOURROAN
SEETO  FIGS  RST
EDSELS  SEAM
  OOZE  SCAMS
COLTSPELL  DRAWS
AREAS  BRONCSZOO
RENTA  ROLE  HERO
YODEL  AYLA  LET
```

49

```
SELF  SOAK  MOSHE
AXEL  ANTIMATTER
RENO  GOLDIEHAWN
ARA  FARADS  EPEE
STOPON  SOPH  LRS
OILIEST  LOWEST
TOILS  MOHAIR
ANNA  CASEY  IMET
 TAUNTS  STEVE
ASSETS  ACCEDES
DEL  OPEN  LARIAT
AMES  INAJAM  CRI
GEENADAVIS  JADE
ELVISSTAMP  ARES
SEEPS  ELIS  GENT
```

50

```
DOS  ALOT  FDS
EXTS  ATARI  TREK
DIRTYDOZEN  RIFE
ADELAIDE  SEGUE
LAW  RED  ATOMIST
USI  DUSTYRHODES
SENT   REOIL
 GREASYSPOON
  ALTOS  SIRS
MUDDYWATERS  CEL
UNRESTS  LOP  OSO
SWEDE  NITRATES
KIWI  FILTHYRICH
ISIN  AGEES  ANTE
EEN  DORS  ESS
```

51

```
DUCT  ALAMO  ESTA
OSHA  GRAIN  PAST
GUARDHOUSE  IFAT
MARTIAN  DISCERN
ALTAR  BOSKET
 REPRO  MINYAN
SITE  RIND  REPLY
ERA  CON  ART  ITE
MOCHA  KITE  SNIT
INKERS  CABLE
 LAOTSE  ANSEL
ACERBIC  SKITTLE
SOBS  CENTERFOLD
TROT  KNEEL  OLEG
INXS  STOMP  RENE
```

52

```
SPECS  SALE  AQUA
EGRET  EROS  SUNS
EAGLESCOUT  TITI
 REAMS  DACIA
SHANANA  HARKEN
DEAREST  GIL  SDS
OMITS  BIKINI
AIRS  DOONE  ELLA
 TYPING  CAVER
PER  ESS  PORTENT
ELIJAH  JUNIORS
SAGES  CURLS
CIGS  HOKEYPOKEY
ONES  EKES  ELITE
WERE  WEST  RENEW
```

53

```
ROALD  LARDS  BBS
AUDIO  ANAME  OUI
ZZZZZZZZZZZZZZZ
ZOE  EIEIO  OOZE
  CNN  ORDER
 HIRSCH  DROOL
PANE  AUSTRALIA
SSSSSSSSSSSSSSS
SPECTATOR  TEAS
STEAL  SEVENS
 NYETS  BAR
BIND  WHORL  FIR
OOOOOOOOOOOOOOO
OWE  WHOOP  UNITS
PAL  LOFTS  RELAY
```

54

```
GAGA  ALES  BUDS
EGAN  ARENT  ASEA
TILT  PUTSONHOLD
ILL  VENTURA
TEENER  REDACT
 YEN  MAE  INOR
TAPEDECK  PADRES
LORD  SLIER  ODES
CROFTS  STERNEST
TOUR  SSA  ALL
AFLAME  STYLES
 IODATES  HUT
TAKINGABOW  LUBE
EPIC  UTURN  ELIE
DOTE  LETS  SLED
```

55

```
ARE  ABBY  PASDE
DEM  BARA  OUTLET
ICE  DRAWINGCARD
MARQUEENAME  TIS
ENGULF  METRES
ATEE  OAF  EDIE
 EMOTES  ASTOR
MAINATTRACTIONS
ANNIE  ANGLED
STUN  SEE  USAF
 INGOOD  RUANDA
THD  STARBILLING
HEADLINEACT  DAG
ARTIES  AJAR  ETE
TOERR  LALA  RED
```

56

```
BURGS  LAIC  BLIP
ISAAC  ANNA  RAVE
FIZZIOLOGY  IDEA
FAZE  RAN  ERNEST
   TSE  SNUG
 AUTHORDONTURE
OSTEO  EINE  PEND
UPI  RECROSS  LIE
RICH  GOER  ASIDE
 CAIROPRACTICS
   COTY  HEN
GRUCCI  OWE  GRIT
LULU  SIGHTOLOGY
ASAP  TORE  LETON
DENS  SUEY  ADORE
```

57

```
C O C A · P A S S · M A K O
A M O S · T O N I C · A R I D
T A R T · O L D E R · R E D D
C H E R R Y Y O G U R T · · ·
H A D I T · · R E B O I L E D
· · D E S K · · S N I D E · ·
L O B E · P A P P Y Y O K U M
A B E · A T R I A · E C O
Y E A R B Y Y E A R · A D E S
E S T E E · · S N O B · · · ·
R E S O L U T E · · R A I L S
· · · C A N A R Y Y E L L O W
T A L C · I L I A D · O L G A
A L O U · T I C K S · N E A L
B L U R · S A S S · E R N E
```

58

```
S I T U P · A C T S · F A O
A L O N G · P L A I T · A L P
C L E A R H E A D E D · I L E
· · · W A I T S · · E R R O R
L O C A T E S · C A N A S T A
A Z O R E S · S H R I N K · ·
D O L E D · T H A T S · I S A
E N D S · F I E R Y · G N U S
D E B · H I L L Y · R A N T S
· · L I O N E L · C E T E R A
S P O O L E D · B A G H D A D
I R O N Y · · T O R R E · · ·
R O D · W A R M H E A R T E D
E V E · A R O A R · D E E R E
N E D · R E I N · E D N A S
```

59

```
D A D A · D E F E R · O F I T
A M I S · O L I V E · V I V A
I M A F I R M B E L I E V E R
S O L A C E S · · · C R E S T
· · · T O M · H A W E D · · ·
I N F A M I L Y V A L U E S
P A R S E · O M I T · B L A B
S O I · A N N A S · E L I
E M M A · G E A R · A S N O T
I L L S E L L Y O U M I N E
· · · L A D Y S · F R A · · ·
A B O O K · · · A R A L S E A
F O R F I F T Y D O L L A R S
A D A M · G R O O M · E G O S
R Y N E · H A N S E · R E S T
```

60

```
S O S · P R O · R A D I A N
C H I · S H O W · O N E O U T
R A T · H I D E A N D S I K H
A R O M A · · N E A P · · · ·
G A N D H I C A N E · O N C E
· · I S D O N E · S T O O L
O V A · E R A · T R I C K Y
D E L H I S A N D W I C H E S
E X T O R T · G E O · E S E
T E A M S · S E A B E D · ·
O D I E · J O L L Y R A J A H
· · B E A U · · I N U R E · ·
A G R A C U L T U R E · D I G
P O I S O N · S K I S · G E E
R O D E N T · K E G · E L L
```

61

```
E M P T Y · W E P T · L I A R
L O U I E · A M O S · A L T E
E N T E R A N E L E C T I O N
M A S C · G E R E · S T A L E
· · · L A R R Y · N E E D L E
A R M A D A S · B O A R · · ·
R O U S E · C E L · M A I
C O M P E T E O N A T R A C K
S D S · E S Q · H E N C E
· · · S E E S · T E A P O T S
E V E N T S · M A N I A · · ·
L O G A N · M A R V · I S T O
M I G R A T E U P S T R E A M
E L E E · B O N O · B E R R A
R A D S · S W A N · A R B O R
```

62

```
L A S T · U S E R · S A P I D
E C H O · N O L O · P R A D O
T H E N O B L E S T O F A L L
M E D I C O · N E R O · R Y E
E D S · T R E A S O N · · ·
· · M O N A · U S M A I L
A T E U P · R A N G · E N D E
D O G S I S T H E H O T D O G
A T O I · C H A R · U R A L S
H O N C H O · V E T O · ·
· · · I T F E E D S · T H E
C H E · N C O S · D E M E A N
H A N D T H A T B I T E S I T
O L D I E · M E R E · A L T E
P O S E D · Y E A S · L A I R
```

63

```
S P R E A D · J A M S · A D D
A I E L L O · I D E A · L E E
I N S I D E · G O L D L E A F
L A T H E S · · L A X L Y · ·
· · · U R N S · S T E W · · ·
D E E R S T A L K E R · W E D
A R L O · T O A D · B I D E
I N T O · E D I T S · U Z I S
R I O T · T O R E · D E C K
Y E N · P O W E R P L A N T S
· · · P E N N · S H E B · · ·
P U M A S · · R A B B I T · ·
S T E M T U R N · A V O U C H
S A D · E S A U · S E T T E E
T H E · R E N T · E N T E R O
```

64

```
· L A M B · C B E R · S A S S
R O D E O · R E L Y · O N T O
O C E A N · O G L E · U T A H
S A L T S A W A Y · P R E G O
A L E · A I N T · P E G · ·
· · S I R · · B A R R O O M
S T E W · S T A R S · A M M O
A R T E · T R E E S · P A I N
K I T E · R E C A P · E R T E
S P U T N I K · O K S · ·
· · T O P · D A R E · B I O
M A J O R · B I T T E R E N D
O L E O · G O A L · P O L L O
D A R T · A N N A · U T T E R
S I K H · B E E S · P E S T
```

65

```
J A M B · V I C A R · H O B O
E L A L · E N O L A · E V E R
D E M I · R I D O F · N I L E
I C A N N O T A F F O R D T O
· · · T I N · · · T I D Y · ·
Q U I Z K I D S · A D V I S E
A S H E · C U E D · L I N U S
T A E · W A S T E M Y · C A T
A G A T E · T U B A · L O V E
R E R E A D · P I L L A G E S
· · L I R A · · · I A N · · ·
T I M E M A K I N G M O N E Y
O N Y X · M E L O N · L O P E
O G R E · A L E N E · I D E A
L E A D · S A T E D · N E E R
```

66

```
L A D · N O R A D · A C E D
I C E D · E L A T E · S U R E
M A C E B E A R E R · C R I B
P R O B E D · E T A · O R E S
· · · A G E S · E N J O Y · ·
P E C T O R A L · G O L F E R
I N L E T · V A L E T · A M I
A T O R · P E P Y S · E V I L
N E V · E R R O R · S T O L E
O R E L S E · F E S T E R E D
· · N I E C E · S A A R · · ·
R A F T · E X O · T I N G E D
A L O T · D I L L Y D A L L Y
V I O L · E L D E R · L O B E
E T T E · D E E D S · W A D
```

67

```
J O S E · H E L P S · M O M A
E A T S · E L E N I · A N E W
T R A P A F O X I N A H O L E
E S T A B · · N A N A · · · ·
· · · N I O B E · I N T R O S
B R O A D C A S T · E M E R Y
R E O · E A R T H A · A G I N
A F L · D L I · I L L · G A T
Q U I P · A N G E L O · A N A
U N T I L · G I V E T H E A X
E D E N I C · G E N I E · · ·
· · · · E T R E · · O C U L O
U S E T H E S P R I N K L E R
Z A S U · S A I N T · L A N E
I T E M · T I N A S · E N O S
```

68

```
· B A S E S · · · S A G E S T
S A M P L E R · S C U L L E D
A R E A W A Y · O R D A I N S
S I X W A S A F R A I D · · ·
· · · N Y C · R E M · I D A
B R A S · A P E R · J O I N S
L A S · E P E E · R O L L I E
O F S E V E N · B E C A U S E
A T O N E S · L A C K · T E D
T E R M S · T O T E · B E S S
· · · R T E · O H O · P E A
· · · S E V E N A T E N I N E
F I G H T E R · D I L A T O R
I N T E R N E · E V E N I N G
G E O D E S · · · E R A S E
```

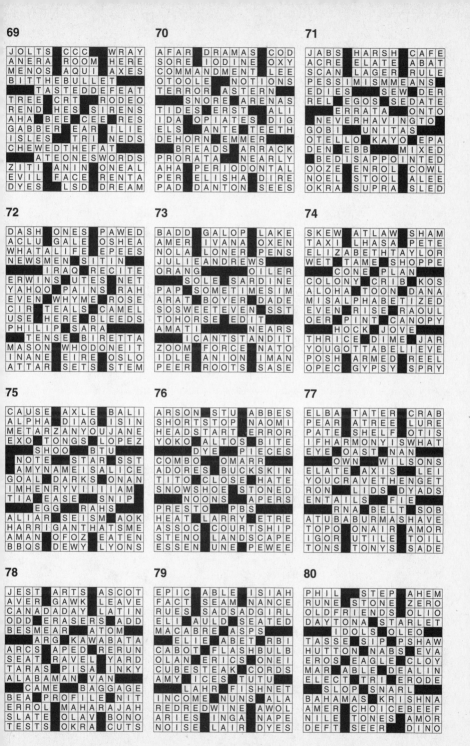

69

```
JOLTS  CCC  WRAY
ANERA  ROOM HERE
MENOS  AQUI AXES
BITTHEBULLET
    TASTEDDEFEAT
TREE CRT  RODEO
REND HES  SIRENS
AHA BEE CEE  RES
GABBER EAR  ILIE
ISLES  TRI  NEDS
CHEWEDTHEFAT
ATEONESWORDS
ZITI ANIN  ONEAL
EVIL FACE  RENTA
DYES LSD   DREAM
```

70

```
AFAR DRAMAS  COD
SORE IODINE  OXY
COMMANDMENT  LEE
OTOOLE  NOTIONS
TERROR  ASTERN
   SNORE ARENAS
TIDES ERST  ALI
IDA OPIATES  DIG
ELS ANTE  TEETH
DEHORN  EMMER
   BREADS ARRACK
PRORATA  NEARLY
AHA PERIODONTAL
PER ELISHA  DIRE
PAD DANTON  SEES
```

71

```
JABS HARSH  CAFE
ACRE ELATE  ABAT
SCAN LAGER  RULE
PESSIMISMMEANS
EDIES  SEW  DER
REL EGOS  SEDATE
   ERRATA  ONTO
NEVERHAVINGTO
GOBI   UNITAS
OTELLO KAYO  EPA
DEN EBB   MIXED
BEDISAPPOINTED
OOZE ENROL  COWL
NOEL STOOL  ALEE
OKRA SUPRA  SLED
```

72

```
DASH ONES  PAWED
ACLU GALE  OSHEA
WHATALIFE  EPEES
NEWSMEN  SITIN
   IRAQ  RECITE
ERWINS UTES  NET
YAHOO PAINS  RAH
EVEN WHYME  ROSE
CIR TEALS  CAMEL
USE HERE  BLEEDS
PHILIP  SARA
   TENSE BIRETTA
MASON WHODONEIT
INANE EIRE  OSLO
ATTAR SETS  STEM
```

73

```
BADD GALOP  LAKE
AMER IVANA  OXEN
NOLA LONER  PENS
JULIEANDREWS
ORANG   OILER
   SOLE SARDINE
PAP SOMETIMESIM
ARAT BOYER  DADE
SOSWEETEVEN SST
TOHORSE  EDIT
AMATI   NEARS
ICANTSTANDIT
ZOOM FORCE  NATO
IDLE ANION  IMAN
PEER ROOTS  SASE
```

74

```
SKEW ATLAW  SHAM
TAXI LHASA  PETE
ELIZABETHTAYLOR
WET TAME  SHOPPE
   CONE   PLAN
COLONY CRIB  KOS
ALOHA TOON  DANA
MISALPHABETIZED
EVEN RISE  RAOUL
OER PINT  CANOPY
   HOCK   JOVE
THRICE DIME  JAR
YOUGOTTABELIEVE
POSH ARMED  REEL
OPEC GYPSY  SPRY
```

75

```
CAUSE  AXLE  BALI
ALPHA  DIAG  ISIN
METARZANYOUJANE
EXO TONGS  LOPEZ
   SHOO   BTU
NOTE  STAR  SST
AMYNAMEISALICE
GOAL DARKS  ONAN
IMHENRYVIIIIAM
TIA EASE   SNIP
   EGG    RAHS
ALIAR SEISM  AOK
HARRIGANTHATSME
AMAN OFOZ  EATEN
BBQS DEWY  LYONS
```

76

```
ARSON STU  ABBES
SHORTSTOP  NAOMI
HEADSTART  ERROR
YOKO ALTOS  BITE
   DYE  PIECES
COMBO  OMARR
ADORES  BUCKSKIN
TITO CLOSE  HATE
SNOWSHOE  STONED
NOONS  APERS
PRESTO  PBS
HEAT LARRY  ETRE
ASSOC  COURTSHIP
STENO  LANDSCAPE
ESSEN UNE  PEWEE
```

77

```
ELBA TATER  CRAB
PEAR ATREE  LURE
PATE SHELF  OTIS
IFHARMONYISWHAT
EYE OAST   NAN
   OWN  WILSONS
ELATE AXIS   LEI
YOUCRAVETHENGET
RON LIDS  DYADS
ENTAILS   FIE
   RNA BELT  SOB
ATUBABURMASHAVE
TOPO ONAIR  AMOR
IGOR UTILE  TOIL
TONS TONYS  SADE
```

78

```
JEST ARTS  ASCOT
AVER GAWK  LEAVE
CANADADAY  LATIN
ODD ERASERS  ADD
BESMEAR   ATOM
   ARG KAWABATA
ARCS APED  RERUN
SEAT RAVEL  YARD
TARAS PISA  INKY
ALABAMAN   VAN
   CAME BAGGAGE
BEA PROFILE  NIT
ERROL MAHARAJAH
SLATE OLAV  BONO
TESTS OKRA  CUTS
```

79

```
EPIC ABLE  ISIAH
FACT SEAM  NANCE
RUES SADSADGIRL
ELI AULD  SEATED
MACABRE   ASPS
   ELIE ABET RBI
CABOT FLASHBULB
OLAN ERICS  ONEI
CUBESTEAK  CORDS
AMY ICES  TUTU
   LAHR FISHNET
INCOME NUNS  ALA
REDREDWINE  AWOL
ARIES INGA  NAPE
NOISE LAIR  DYES
```

80

```
PHIL  STEP  AHEM
RUNE STONE  ZERO
OLDFRIENDS  OLIO
DAYTONA  STARLET
   IDOLS   OLEO
TASSE SIP  PSHAW
HUTTON NABS  EVA
EROS EAGLE  CLOY
MAR ABLE  DEALIN
ELECT TRI  ERODE
   SLOP   SNARL
BAHAMAS  KRISHNA
AMER CHOICEBEEF
NILE TONES  AMOR
DEFT SEER   DINO
```

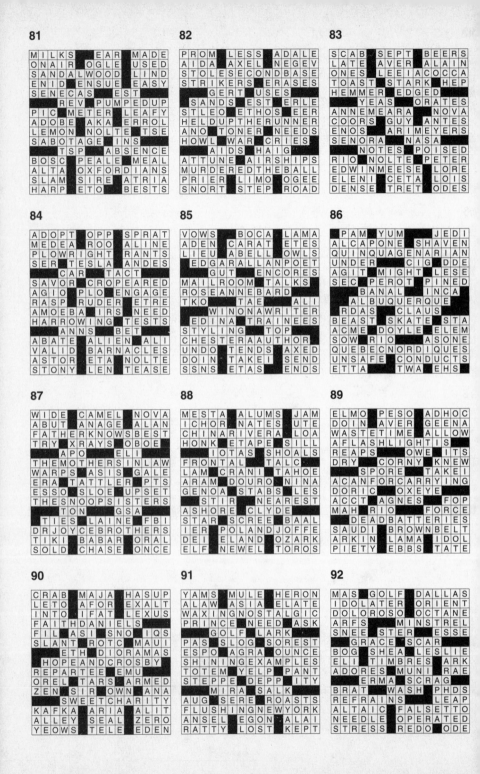

81

```
MILKS   EAR   MADE
ONAIR  OGLE   USED
SANDALWOOD    LIND
ENID  ENSUE   EASY
SENECAS    EST
    REV  PUMPEDUP
PIC  METER   LEAFY
ADOBE  AKA   ERROL
LEMON  NOLTE   TSE
SABOTAGE   INS
    TSP   ABSENCE
BOSC  PEALE   MEAL
ALTA  OXFORDIANS
SLAM  SIRE   ATRIA
HARP  ETO   BESTS
```

82

```
PROM   LESS   ADALE
AIDA   AXEL   NEGEV
STOLESECONDBASE
STRIKERS    ERASES
    GERT    USES
SANDS   EST   ERLE
STLEO  ETHOS   EER
HELDUPTHERUNNER
ANO   TONER   NEEDS
HOWL   WAR   CRIES
    AIDS   HAIG
ATTUNE   AIRSHIPS
MURDEREDTHEBALL
PRIER   LIMO   OGEE
SNORT   STEP   ROAD
```

83

```
SCAB   SEPT   BEERS
LATE   AVER   ALAIN
ONES   LEEIACOCCA
TOAST   STARK   HEP
HEMMER   EDGED
    YEAS   ORATES
ANNEMEARA    NOVA
COORS   GUY   ANTES
ENOS    ARIMEYERS
SENORA   NASA
    NOTES   POISED
RIO   NOLTE   PETER
EDWINMEESE   LORE
ELENI   CETA   LOIS
DENSE   TRET   ODES
```

84

```
ADOPT   OPP   SPRAT
MEDEA   ROO   ALINE
PLOWRIGHT   RANTS
SER   TESLA   ANDES
    CAR   TACT
SAVOR   CROPEARED
AGIO   PLO   ENGAGE
RASP   RUDER   ETRE
AMOEBA   IRS   NEED
HARROWING   TESTS
    ANNS   BET
ABATE   ALIEN   ALI
VALID   BARNACLES
ASTOR   ETA   NOLTE
STONY   LEN   TEASE
```

85

```
VOWS   BOCA   LAMA
ADEN   CARAT   ETES
LIEU   ABELL   OWLS
EDGARALLANPOET
    GUT   ENCORES
MAILROOM   TALKS
ROSEANNEBARD
TKO    TAE    ALI
  WINONAWRITER
EDINA   TRAINEES
STYLING    TOP
CHESTERAAUTHOR
UNDO   TENDS   AXED
DOIN   TAKEI   SEND
SSNS   ETAS   ENDS
```

86

```
 PAM   YUM   JEDI
ALCAPONE   SHAVEN
QUINQUAGENARIAN
UNDER   CIG   DDE
AGIT   MIGHT   LESE
SEC   PEROT   PINED
   BANAL   INCA
  ALBUQUERQUE
RDAS   CLAUS
BEAST   SKATE   STA
ACME   DOYLE   ELEM
SOW   RIO   ASONE
QUEBECNORDIQUES
UNSAFE   CONDUCTS
ETTA   TWA   EHS
```

87

```
WIDE   CAMEL   NOVA
ABUT   ANAGE   ALAN
FATHERKNOWSBEST
TRY   XRAYS   OBOE
   APO   ELI
THEMOTHERSINLAW
WARPS   ASIS   GALE
ERA   TATTLER   PTS
ESSO   SLOE   UPSET
THESNOOPSISTERS
    TON   GSA
TIES   LAINE   FBI
DRJOYCEBROTHERS
TIKI   BABAR   ORAL
SOLD   CHASE   ONCE
```

88

```
MESTA   ALUMS   JAM
ICHOR   NATES   UTE
CHINARIVERA   LOA
HONK   ETAPE   SILL
    IOTAS   SHOALS
FRONTAL   TALC
LAM   CRANI   TAHOE
ARAM   DOURO   NINA
GENOA   STABS   LES
    STIR   NEAREST
ASHORE   CLYDE
STAR   SCREE   BAAL
IER   POLANDJOFFE
DEI   ELAND   OZARK
ELF   NEWEL   TOROS
```

89

```
ELMO   PESO   ADHOC
DOIN   AVER   GEENA
WASTETIME   ALLOW
AFLASHLIGHTIS
REAPS   OWE   ITS
DRY   CORNY   KNEW
   SPORE   TAKEI
ACANFORCARRYING
DORIC   OXEYE
ACCT   AGNES   FOP
MAH   RIO   FORCE
 DEADBATTERIES
SAUDI   BROWNBELT
ARKIN   LAMA   IDOL
PIETY   EBBS   TATE
```

90

```
CRAB   MAJA   HASUP
LETO   AFOR   EXALT
INTO   IFAT   LEXUS
FAITHDANIELS
FIL   ASI   SNO   IQS
SLANT   ROTC   MAUI
   ETH   DIORAMAS
HOPEANDCROSBY
REPARTEE   EMU
OREL   TARS   ARMED
ZEN   SIR   OWN   ANA
  SWEETCHARITY
KAFKA   ARIA   ALIT
ALLEY   SEAL   ZERO
YEOWS   TELE   EDEN
```

91

```
YAMS   MULE   HERON
ALAW   ASIA   ELATE
WAXINGNOSTALGIC
PRINCE   NEED   ASK
   GOLF   LARK
PAS   SLOG   SOREST
ESPO   AGRA   OUNCE
SHININGEXAMPLES
TOTEM   YELP   PANT
STEPPE   DEPP   ITY
   MIRA   SALK
AUG   SERE   ROASTS
FLUSHINGNEWYORK
ANSEL   EGON   ALAI
RATTY   LOST   KEPT
```

92

```
MAS   GOLF   DALLAS
IDOLATER   ORIENT
DOLOROSO   OCTANE
ARFS    MINSTREL
SNEE   STER   ESSE
  GRACE   SCAR
BOG   SHEA   LESLIE
ELI   TIMBRES   ARK
ADORES   MUNI   RAE
   ERMA   SCRAG
BRAT   WASH   PHDS
REFRAINS   LEAP
ALTAIC   FALSETTO
NEEDLE   OPERATED
STRESS   REDO   ODE
```

93

R	P	M			B	L	O	W	I	T		W	A	T
M	E	A	N		E	A	T	E	R	Y		I	D	O
S	P	R	I	N	G	S	T	E	E	N		N	U	N
	E	X	P	O				N	E	A	T	L	Y	
		P	R	O	B	A	T	E		L	E	T	S	
D	U	T	Y		D	E	L	I		W	A	R		
I	C	H		I	N	A	T		O	N	T	H	E	
O	L	E		G	E	T	B	A	C	K		H	O	W
R	A	F	E	R		S	A	N	E		U	S	E	
	A	L	E		E	M	I	L		A	R	E	S	
I	L	L	S		E	N	A	C	T	E	D			
S	O	L	E	I	L			M	A	I	N			
E	G	G		D	O	N	N	A	S	U	M	M	E	R
E	A	U		O	P	I	A	T	E		S	A	V	E
A	N	Y		L	E	A	N	E	R		N	A	B	

94

B	L	O	W		S	I	N	K			R	I	G	S
Y	O	D	A		C	R	U	E			E	D	N	A
E	X	A	M		H	A	M	E	L		D	E	A	L
			P	I	N	E	B	L	U	F	F	A	R	K
A	C	U	R	A					N	B	A			
P	A	L	M	S	P	R	I	N	G	S	C	A		
O	R	E			S	I	N	E	S		E	R	M	A
T	O	R	S			S	T	E			D	R	A	T
S	N	I	T		W	E	E	D	S			E	M	T
			C	E	D	A	R	R	A	P	I	D	S	I	A
	E	E	N					R	O	U	T	E		
O	A	K	R	I	D	G	E	T	E	N	N			
A	R	E	A		S	O	N	I	A		C	U	J	O
R	I	N	G		B	I	N	D		E	G	O	S	
S	A	T	E		I	D	E	S		S	H	E	S	

95

A	N	T	I		A	D	A	M			S	C	A	B
M	O	O	N		N	I	N	E	S		P	A	S	O
P	R	O	P	A	G	A	N	D	A		A	N	T	S
S	A	L	U	T	E			E	L	A	S	T	I	C
			T	E	L	E	C	A	S	T		E	N	S
H	U	P			E	V	A			A	B	E	L	
E	R	I	C		S	I	N	S		A	G	O	O	D
A	S	C	O	T			L	S	U		Y	O	U	R	E
P	A	C	E	R		S	E	N	S		S	P	A	N
S	T	D		A	D	A	R		C	U	T		E	L	Y
			C	A	N	O	P	I	E	S				
C	H	I	N	E	S	E			G	R	A	T	I	S
R	E	L	Y		P	A	R	A	M	E	D	I	C	S
I	D	L	E		S	T	E	L	A		A	L	O	T
M	A	Y	S			O	D	E	S		T	E	N	S

96

A	B	C	S		S	H	A	M	U		L	A	Z	E
B	O	U	T		N	O	L	A	N		O	M	A	N
B	A	S	E	B	A	L	L	D	I	A	M	O	N	D
A	R	T		L	I	E	S		V	A	S	E	S	
			O	N	E	L		A	M	E	N			
J	A	M	E	S	S	P	A	D	E	R		R	E	S
E	L	M	O	S		E	L	V	I	S		E	L	I
A	L	A		A	R	L	E	N			T	I	D	
N	E	D		E	L	M	E	R		B	R	A	H	E
E	Y	E		J	O	I	N	T	H	E	C	L	U	B
			B	E	E	T			A	L	A	I		
A	D	H	O	C		Z	I	N	C		A	H	A	
H	E	A	R	T	B	R	E	A	K	H	O	T	E	L
A	L	T	O		B	I	N	G	E		N	E	A	P
B	I	E	N		S	P	O	O	R		O	S	L	O

97

F	A	L	L	S		O	G	L	E	D		S	A	W
A	W	A	I	T		F	R	O	M	E		A	R	A
R	A	C	K	E	T	F	A	C	E	S		D	E	N
G	R	E	E	N	E		F	O	R	E	H	A	N	D
O	D	D	S		M	S	T		G	R	E	T	A	S
				A	P	T		S	E	T	S			
B	A	C	K	C	O	U	R	T			T	A	I	L
O	L	L	I	E		F	I	R		A	I	S	L	E
S	A	U	L			F	O	O	T	F	A	U	L	T
			M	I	S	S		K	I	T				
M	E	R	E	S	T		E	E	L		S	C	A	N
O	V	E	R	H	E	A	D		T	R	O	U	P	E
N	E	T		T	E	N	N	I	S	E	L	B	O	W
A	R	R		A	L	T	A	R			A	V	E	R	T
S	T	Y		R	E	E	S	E			P	E	S	T	S

98

C	A	J	U	N		F	L	E	W		A	L	E	C
A	N	I	T	A		L	O	K	I		B	A	J	A
W	O	T	A	N		E	D	E	N		A	P	E	S
		T	H	E	R	E	I	S	N	O	S	U	C	H
A	T	E		T	U	T			I	N	E	P	T	
B	E	R	A	T	E		P	E	P	Y	S			
A	M	B	L	E		C	O	D	E	X		C	U	P
S	P	U	E		T	H	I	N	G		B	O	H	R
H	O	G		L	H	A	S	A		P	I	Q	U	E
			K	E	E	N	E		T	E	N	U	R	E
O	L	I	V	A		B	A	T		I	A	N		
A	S	A	L	I	T	T	L	E	D	U	L	L		
B	A	U	M		E	R	I	N		N	O	L	A	N
O	G	R	E		R	A	Z	E		I	S	E	R	E
Y	E	A	R		S	P	A	T		A	S	S	E	T

99

M	A	T	S		T	R	O	T		L	O	A	N	S
A	L	I	T		R	E	N	E		I	N	D	I	A
S	O	L	O		I	B	I	S		T	O	O	T	S
C	U	T	O	F	B	U	T	T	E	R		G	A	S
			P	I	E	S			L	E	N	O		
F	I	F	E	R	S		A	B	S	O	R	B	S	
A	N	O	D	E		S	I	N	O		D	A	R	T
M	O	O		S	E	T	D	O	W	N		C	U	E
E	N	D	S		L	E	O	N		O	R	A	T	E
R	E	C	O	R	D	S		D	I	E	T	E	R	
			O	B	I	E		S	A	S	E			
A	G	O		F	R	U	I	T	C	E	N	T	E	R
B	I	K	E	L		S	T	A	R		T	O	B	E
A	L	E	N	E		N	E	R	O		E	G	A	N
B	A	R	E	D		A	M	E	N		R	A	N	D

100

S	A	S		D	R	A	B	S		A	N	J	O	U
E	L	O		R	A	D	O	N		S	E	A	L	S
L	I	L		S	H	O	W	O	F	H	A	N	D	S
M	A	E	V	E			S	U	E	T				
A	S	S	A	U	L	T		T	A	R	I	F	F	
			U	N	S	E	A	T		R	A	D	I	A	L
L	A	P		S	A	R	I	S		Y	E	N	T	A
E	X	P	O		P	I	E	T	A		A	G	A	R
A	L	O	N	G		Q	U	A	K	E		E	L	K
H	E	R	O	E	S		P	R	I	M	E	R		
	S	T	R	E	E	P		K	N	E	E	P	A	D
			W	E	A	K			R	E	A	C	H	
M	O	U	T	H	P	I	E	C	E	S		I	T	O
O	M	A	N	I		N	E	A	T	O		N	O	T
M	E	R	T	Z		E	L	L	E	N		T	R	I

PORTABLE, AFFORDABLE CROSSWORDS *from* RANDOM HOUSE

Each selection features 100 fun and easy crosswords presented in a convenient package. These puzzles are sure to delight anyone who's on the go or just on a break. Wherever you plan to be, make sure you have one of these portable volumes by your side.

RANDOM HOUSE BACK TO THE BEACH CROSSWORDS | **$6.95**
RANDOM HOUSE BEDTIME CROSSWORDS | **$6.95**
RANDOM HOUSE BY THE FIRESIDE CROSSWORDS | **$6.95**
RANDOM HOUSE COZY CROSSWORDS | **$6.95**
RANDOM HOUSE MORE VACATION CROSSWORDS | **$6.95**
RANDOM HOUSE VACATION CROSSWORDS | **$6.95**